LINE OF DUTY

DUTY

THE REAL STORY

WENSLEY CLARKSON has investigated numerous crimes across the world for the past thirty years and exposed many criminals and crooked police officers. His research has included prison visits, surveillance operations, police raids and even post-mortems. Clarkson's books – published in more than thirty countries – have sold more than 2 million copies. He has made numerous documentaries in the UK, US, Australia and Spain, and written TV and movie screenplays. Clarkson's recent book, *Sexy Beasts* – about the infamous Hatton Garden heist – was nominated for a Crime Writers' Association Dagger Award.

www.wensleyclarkson.com

Praise for the author

'This is a lurid tale… yet Clarkson tells it in a way that makes it nothing short of fascinating.'
Independent on Sunday on *Bindon*

'Utterly compelling.'
Evening Standard on *Hit 'Em Hard*

'A thrilling glimpse into a hidden world of money, power, glamour and violence.'
Sun on *Killing Charlie*

'Reveals a fascinating life, albeit savage and ultimately wasted.'
Loaded on *Killer on the Road*

'Bindon emerges from Clarkson's portrait as a true gent, if a ferociously violent one, with an unsettling sense of humour.'
Daily Telegraph on *Bindon*

'Sensational stuff.'
Sun on *The Crossing*

LINE OF DUTY

THE REAL STORY

INSIDE BRITISH POLICE CORRUPTION

WENSLEY CLARKSON

JOHN BLAKE

Published by John Blake Publishing,
80–1 Wimpole Street,
Marylebone
London W1G 9RE

www.facebook.com/johnblakebooks
twitter.com/jblakebooks

This edition first published in 2020

Paperback ISBN: 978-1-78946-341-5
eBook ISBN: 978-1-78946-342-2
Audio ISBN: 978-1-78946-370-5

British Library Cataloguing-in-Publication Data:

A catalogue record for this book is available from the British Library.

Design by www.envydesign.co.uk

Printed and bound in Great Britain by Clays Ltd, Elcograf S.p.A.

1 3 5 7 9 10 8 6 4 2

John Blake Publishing is an imprint of Bonnier Books UK
www.bonnierbooks.co.uk

Many real-life crimes – including murder – have been committed by the UK's corrupt police. So to all the families of their victims I say, 'You're not forgotten.'

AUTHOR'S NOTE

The words were scrawled on a blank page inside one of my bestselling true crime books, sent to me by an underworld contact. The note read: '*Wensley Clarkson has printed loads of lies about me in his books and caused untold damage. The tables will turn one day.*'

The gangster who wrote this chilling threat is an infamous UK crime boss, who sees himself as invincible because he allegedly has so many corrupt police officers in his pocket. He was angry at my efforts to expose the role of some of his favourite crooked coppers in a notorious murder.

This particular police corruption case revolved around a cold-blooded killing that shocked this nation and continues to cause outrage and disgust more than a quarter of a century later. And despite almost forty years of allegedly bribing the police, this same gang boss who threatened me has never actually been prosecuted for any offence linked to police corruption.

Today, Scotland Yard's Directorate of Professional Standards (DPS) – originally called A10 before becoming CIB1, then CIB2 – is the modern-day, real-life equivalent of TV's *Line of Duty* AC-12 anti-corruption unit.

In the past, such anti-corruption units have earned nicknames like 'Ghost Squad' and 'The Untouchables', their detectives known as the 'rubber heels' because of the unobtrusive way in which they had to operate. In days gone by, officers on these specialised units were even dismissively described by many cynical colleagues in other departments as 'The Muppets'.

Other UK forces also have their own versions of Scotland Yard's DPS, although smaller, provincial forces tend to pool their resources, and in today's supposedly more open atmosphere, the existence of such units is now well known.

In *Line of Duty: The Real Story* I've used the success of the unique TV drama series to highlight the murky world of real-life police corruption, which so often gets swept under the carpet.

I've been writing true-crime books for more than thirty years and in that time I've met criminals of all shapes and sizes. But my encounters with crooked police officers were often the most chilling. They're virtually impossible to interview openly, so, on some occasions, I've had to secretly tape record their confessions and even that was a risky enterprise because many of them were clearly prone to violence. One so-called bent copper got so paranoid that he pushed me against a wall and started frisking me, only to stop when one of his colleagues intervened.

On the 'official' police side, it's clear that many officers find it hard even in this day and age to come to terms with the corruption that has existed within the UK's police services for many generations. As a result, a lot of police officers try to avoid the subject like the plague. Retired officers even fear losing their police pensions if they speak out. Therefore, some events in this book have been dramatised in order to protect incidents and the identities of the individuals concerned.

Even those officers who've done nothing whatsoever wrong were reluctant to contribute officially to this book. As one put it: 'Corruption is such a grey area inside the police. Many would say there was no smoke without fire if any officer talked openly about it.'

No wonder then that TV's *Line of Duty* has played such a pivotal role in helping to 'educate' normal law-abiding citizens about the real-life crooked officers in our midst. Such activities are now a talking point for millions of fans of the show.

Some gangsters I interviewed claimed that crooked cops actually posed a bigger threat to their lives than any rival criminals. One explained: 'Crooked cops tend to be cold-blooded bastards. It comes with the territory. If you cross 'em, they come back at you really viciously and they've got the power of the police behind them.

'That means they can even put you away if you upset them. Also, bent cops can get their own gangster mates to pay you a visit. No wonder villains are not keen on grassing them up.'

In this book we'll examine the character traits of real-life police officers alongside the intricate backstories constructed by creator Jed Mercurio for his *Line of Duty* investigators to make them believable to a TV audience.

Police officers in the real world are supposed to abide by the law and operate to a set of rules that's designed to protect and serve the public. But *Line of Duty: The Real Story* exposes what happens when they turn into the perpetrators of crime.

Wensley Clarkson
London, 2020

CONTENTS

CAST OF CHARACTERS

Without them, the disturbing real-life stories of police corruption wouldn't exist.

SPIDER – Drugs were the route of his evil

GREY FOX – Camouflaged all his bungs (bribes)
TRIGGER – Always treading on dangerous ground

SHARK – Swam deep and came up smelling of roses

JACKAL – Cold-blooded killer addicted to murder

JOEY BOY – Played them all off against each other

GRINDER – Turned the tables on his enemies

EMPEROR OF PORN – Always greased the right palms
GREENO – A classic copper's copper

LINE OF DUTY: THE REAL STORY

TROUBLE – Turned an entire city into the UK's gun capital

CHIEF TOM – Bent the rules to his own advantage

BADGER – High-tech inside man

THE PI – Tried to expose the bad apples

DENT – Paid the ultimate price

DEV – Haunted by a life of crime

FAT KEN – Ate one lunch too many

FOXY – Headed for the hills when facing exposure

BUNTER – Turned a friendship into a business

BERTIE – Supergrass from hell

BIFFO – A real-life Ted Hastings

FRED – Hash baron on a high

TAFFY – The most tragic cop of all

WICKED BILL – Top man at the Dirty Squad
KEV – Grassed up the baddest cops

CAST OF CHARACTERS

SPUD – Starred on the list from hell

LEM – Took the wrong guys for a ride

LOU – The secret policeman

MESUT – A classic 'clean skin'

THE PIMPERNEL – Corrupt cops kept him one step ahead

ANT THE CLEANER – Caught in the deadly crossfire

DREADS – Knows the City of Gold inside out

SPEEDY – A bad cop in jail who thrived

VIRGO – Greed got the better of him

ALI – Thought he was King of the Castle

TANK – Took a gamble to save his life

KEL – Bent cop spearheading a deadly trade

Introduction

ROOT OF ALL EVIL

CORRUPTION [uncountable] dishonest or illegal
behaviour, especially of people in authority

The *Concise Oxford English Dictionary* explanation should
really be set in a picture frame hanging on the wall
behind *Line of Duty*'s AC-12 chief Ted Hastings' desk. It gets
right to the heart of the real-life implications of the word
'corruption' and it sums up the tainted world you're about
to enter.

For thousands of years, corruption was usually hidden,
spoken about in hushed tones. Today, many know all about
it, but most take it for granted, even in so-called First
World countries like the UK. In nations around the world,
corruption is a precious commodity that has helped crooked
kings, presidents and prime ministers to acquire great wealth.

Some of those countries even encourage rampant corruption

in order to retain some semblance of law and order. Ironic but true. But there is undoubtedly a relentless and ruthless efficiency to those levels of corruption. The recipients often consider it a necessary tax rather than outright stealing. The larger the amounts of cash involved, the less surprise there is. The fever of corruption is here to stay.

In fact, high-level corruption is now considered an essential ingredient in many societies, often providing a twisted sense of stability in nations verging on civil war.

But what about the type of corruption that's helped turn *Line of Duty* into one of the most successful programmes in UK TV history? Without it, the officers of AC-12 wouldn't have a job. Their dilemma – and that of many real-life police units specifically set up to investigate bent coppers – is that a thin line often exists between real corruption and manipulation when it comes to a police officer and his duties.

That grey area is probably one of the main reasons why *Line of Duty* succeeds so well as a drama format. The investigators have to work their way through myriad problems and implications to get to the truth. Perfect ingredients for a gripping drama.

* * *

There is nothing admirable about the real-life criminal cops you're going to read about here. But it's worth considering that many of them found themselves caught in a no-man's land of hate and resentment.

Some of them even admitted to me they always had a sneaking admiration for the professional criminals of the past, whom many of them had tried to bring to justice before deciding to go crooked. These so-called old-school villains committed crimes like heists and bank robberies and were renowned for their skills and dexterity. Some detectives say that corruption in many ways harks back to that same golden age of crime, when audacity and sheer nerve were the key qualities necessary for those aspiring to acquire rapid criminal wealth.

But today's criminal cops are a different breed altogether. They've used deceit, abuse of power and disloyalty on a massive scale. No wonder they provide the makers of *Line of Duty* with so many 'golden' moments of drama and suspense.

Corrupt officers literally discard their colleagues by turning crooked. And they often put those colleagues in great personal danger as well. For corrupt police officers break the most basic rules of engagement by stitching up their workmates. No wonder most professional criminals hate 'bent coppers' much more than their traditional enemies, the honest members of the long arm of the law.

Typically, corrupt police officers tend to be loners who often come from unsettled childhood home lives. That could mean being born at the rundown end of town where admitting you even wanted to be a police officer was not something you'd share openly with any of your mates.

The characters of real-life crooked cops often revolve around the dynamics of fear and spontaneous, yet controlled violence, or at least the threat of such is omnipresent. Being 'bent' is about balancing brute force with razor sharpness and, most important of all, sheer bloody-minded instinct.

Every eventuality has to be covered. Every threat of exposure must be discarded in case it lands you in the shit or exposes your illicit activities to your superiors. Because when you're out to screw your colleagues just one false move and you're doomed.

A lot of the crooked officers I spoke to insisted they were forced into a corner by circumstances beyond their control and as a result had to turn bad in order to survive. It's a popular excuse for a multitude of sins in life.

Yet many of the UK's most corrupt officers have not only retired without a stain on their characters, but even landed themselves with well-paid assignments for this country's security services, as well as for lawyers, corporations and even the civil service. It's estimated that 25 per cent of the UK's most powerful conglomerates have used the unofficial services of onetime corrupt cops through their lawyers, often without even realising it. That's another cash-driven dilemma for all concerned.

So how was all this real-life police corruption and abuse of power turned into the format for one of the BBC's most successful ever dramas?

When *Line of Duty* was created in 2012, going inside the world of corrupt cops must have seemed quite a risky enterprise to ratings-obsessed executives at the BBC.

Today, the impact this drama series has had on real-life policing in undeniable. Many serving and retired officers I interviewed for this book are convinced it's helped bring the 'problems' of police corruption to the top of the list of priorities for most forces in the UK.

TV industry insiders point to a drama series called *Law & Order* written more than forty years ago for the BBC by former police officer G. F. Newman as being the most likely inspiration for *Line of Duty*. This was a truly groundbreaking drama series that tackled police corruption in a way never before seen on television.

The programme comprised four connected plays and was first transmitted on 6 April 1978 on BBC Two. Each of the four stories within the series was told from a different perspective, including that of the Detective, the Villain, the Brief and the Prisoner. The series sparked controversy on its release because of its depiction of a corrupt British law enforcement and legal system.

G. F. Newman has since stated that he considered '90 per cent of police to be corrupt at the time, and that there has been no significant change since then.'

Other TV drama inspirations for *Line of Duty* no doubt include a number of hit US series featuring police officers who somehow manage to be fully fledged public heroes, despite breaking the law with impunity driven on by their own insane greed. Some of the most successful investigators are often also amongst the most crooked.

Line of Duty cleverly twists this police underworld into a template for a hugely successful TV cop drama. One of the most intriguing and challenging aspects of the series is the way that it also manages to combine new and old-fashioned policing techniques, even inside a modern anti-corruption unit such as AC-12.

The intention of *Line of Duty: The Real Story* is not only

to expose the UK's secret world of corrupt police officers, but also to reveal for the first time the chilling reality that a new breed of corrupt police seems to be gaining a stranglehold inside many police forces across the UK.

And these crooked activities continue to thrive, despite new technology and a supposedly more pro-active attitude towards corruption inside the police force itself.

So what makes a police officer turn bad?

The answers are complex and will shock even the most ardent fans of *Line of Duty*.

But these are the true stories that need to be told.

Chapter One

THE OLD SCHOOL

'I didn't float up the lagoon on a bubble...'
Superintendent Ted Hastings, AC-12

*'Always let me know straight away if you need
anythin' because I know people everywhere. I'm in
a little firm in a firm. If you're nicked anywhere in
London, I can get on the blower to someone in my
firm who will know someone somewhere who will get
somethin' done.'*
**Corrupt real-life London detective John Symonds in a
taped conversation with a London gangster**

BOMBSITES AND BENCH SEATS

One of the few criticisms of *Line of Duty* is that it often
implies that police corruption is a modern problem.
Nothing could be further from the truth.

For more than a century, police officers used their uniforms
and power without impunity to control and bully criminals,

which in turn led to wholesale bribery and corruption. From Victorian times up to the late 1930s, a crooked undercurrent tainted the UK police image of the 'friendly bobby'.

It's often been said that police corruption first came out into the open more than seventy-five years ago on the bombsites of war-torn London. There'd been a vast increase in crimes being committed at the time because most men of a certain age were away fighting in the Second World War. Police resources were so stretched it was easier to 'look the other way' a lot of the time or even charge 'a fee' for doing so.

Many of the UK's most notorious professional criminals of the following decades were born and brought up in wartime London. They went on to participate in some of the most famous crimes of the century, but these legends of the underworld would never forget the local wartime bobbies, who demanded a 'few bob' in exchange for turning a blind eye to a wide assortment of petty crimes.

Many London homes during those war years were run by hard-working womenfolk, struggling around the clock to feed and care for their large broods of children while their husbands were away at war. With no playgrounds and few parks, youngsters ended up larking about on nearby bombsites and desolate wasteland. Local rubbish tips often provided the raw material to make everything from box carts to wooden swords and toy guns.

These characters and their siblings were roaming free from the ages of three or four. Their mothers didn't worry. They were just relieved to get them all out of their tiny homes. As a matter of fact, many of these homes became hubs for local villains, who'd pop round at all times of the day and night to stash their booty under a child's mattresses or in a makeshift bomb shelter built in the back garden.

Inquisitive policemen were slipped a few bob to look the other way and the London underworld quickly went from strength to strength, built on a bedrock of thievery often supported by corrupt police officers.

Back then, a police constable's pay started at sixty-two shillings (£5) a week, with six shillings rent allowance and one shilling boot allowance. Decent digs cost around thirty shillings, and the only alternative was the grim police section house. Many bobbies on the beat were regarded with outright hostility by the poor, and it was hardly surprising since many policemen made free use of 'Johnny Wood' – as they called their truncheons – when not getting a lucrative backhander of cash.

By the 1950s, those gangs of young scallywags on bombsites had evolved into professional criminals or police officers. As one retired Flying Squad detective later explained: 'I decided to become a copper because so many of my mates ended up in borstal. It didn't look glamorous to me. I wanted to keep the streets safe, not steal from people.'

So by the 1950s, it was presumed that 'the cozzers' would continue to be paid off to ignore all dodgy activities. One former bank robber from that era later recalled: 'We took it for granted that most coppers were bent because they were so badly paid and there was nothing wrong with bunging them a few bob now and again.'

These days, many police officers believe that the mentality

born all those years ago helped taint the UK's big city police forces with the never-ending stench of corruption. Another onetime bank robber from south London recalled: 'Some of the bent coppers were alright but others used their power to bully us, even though they were on the take. It made many of us hate them even more back then.'

Many old-school police and criminals have told me about this down the years. But they said that a lot of the crooked officers they dealt with would have seemed harmless these days. 'They only got the odd fiver. Nothing big. But there were always some greedy bastards who'd come back to haunt us later,' recalled one former bank robber. 'They'd get ideas above their station and start lording it around because they knew we had to pay – even if we hated their fuckin' guts – which was more often than not.'

Those corrupt officers seemed to the underworld to be stuck in a time warp. They were in many ways entombed by their own out-dated attitudes towards law and order. They often sneered at their younger colleagues coming through the ranks, who naïvely believed that corruption was like a bad cancer that needed to be forcibly cut out.

BLAGGERS

Many old-time British criminals still look back through rose-tinted glasses to the 'golden age' of armed robbery at least sixty years ago, when 'blaggers' – as armed robbers were known – ruled the streets of the UK's big cities. They were well-drilled *firms* operating with what seemed like military precision.

Often wearing elaborate disguises, or just plain boiler suits, they'd storm banks and hijack cash-in-transit wagons. Working mainly in and around London and other big cities, they netted hundreds of thousands in used notes – and occasionally the odd million or three. But the stakes and sentences were Draconian for those caught, often after being informed on by colleagues who'd swapped information with corrupt detectives in exchange for keeping themselves out of jail.

Many old-school criminals in the UK insist that corrupt cops played a pivotal role in this country's most infamous crime, The Great Train Robbery, which occurred in August 1963. Most of the gang were fairly quickly rounded up by police. They all refused to admit to anything as they believed they might yet be found not guilty at their eventual trial.

On 3 December 1963, one of the ringleaders of the train robbery gang, Charlie Wilson, tried to 'negotiate' his way out of Bedford Prison by offering one senior detective a £50,000 bribe to 'lose' the evidence police had against him. Wilson even claimed he'd been framed for the robbery by corrupt cops, who'd taken his fingerprint samples and ensured a print was then conveniently 'found' on a drum of Saxo salt at the gang's hideout.

To criminals of that era like Charlie Wilson, offering an officer a bribe was nothing particularly out of the ordinary. Fifty thousand pounds in cash was left in a telephone box in Great Dover Street in central London. But the policeman he'd offered the bribe to had already told his superiors. As a result, detectives recovered £50,000 of missing Great Train

Robbery cash, which consisted of notes so mouldy that most of them were stuck together.

However, significantly, Charlie Wilson's attempt at bribing a police officer was not seen as anything out of the ordinary at that time. This clearly implies that wholesale bribery of officers was a common day occurrence then. Some crooked cops were rumoured to even be committing actual crimes themselves in order to line their pockets with tainted cash and cling on to power within police departments. Their colleagues were often too scared to confront them about their corrupt activities.

No one back then seemed prepared to bring these bad cops to justice.

OUT OF CONTROL

'A firm within a firm' was a phrase made infamous by a unit of corrupt cops who were exposed by newspapers back in the early 1970s. And it didn't end there – today there is clear evidence that so-called gangs of renegade police officers have been running crooked operations right under the noses of their colleagues ever since.

In *Line of Duty*, most corrupt cops tend to be 'loner' individuals operating off their own backs, only occasionally in league with other colleagues. But in reality there is clear evidence that for more than fifty years renegade teams of corrupt police officers have been running rings around senior officers, who were often powerless to bring them to justice because of the notorious 'grey areas' connected to allegedly corrupt policing.

One recently retired detective explained: 'Back in the old days, bent cops ran their own "gangs" of corrupt officers and they often expanded in size and power without anyone curtailing them. In fact, most senior officers seemed afraid to take them on.'

No doubt this attitude helped create an ongoing climate of corruption to the point where police chiefs would often shrug their shoulders and allow these renegade officers to thrive on the basis that many of them were also good thief catchers. It was easier to turn a blind eye to corruption allegations because it then helped keep it away from the public eye.

During the 1970s, renegade units of police detectives based in the south-east of England were said to even be offering 'services' from bank robbery to murder to any criminal prepared to pay them enough.

'It sounds outrageous today but that was what it was like back then,' recalled another recently retired detective. 'I remember when I first heard the rumours, I laughed, because I couldn't believe that corrupt police even existed. It all sounded like the figment of a criminal's imagination.'

The same detective continued: 'Then one day I read a front-page newspaper article about a robbery and realised immediately it was the same one that a bunch of my colleagues had been laughing and joking about in a pub a few nights earlier. They'd done it. They'd not just turned rogue, they'd turned into professional criminals.'

And at the centre of all this was one unique police unit synonymous with superb detective work *and* overt corruption.

BRITAIN'S ULTIMATE THIEF-TAKERS

In *Line of Duty*, many of the most infamous real-life UK police departments are never mentioned, most probably for legal reasons. The producers and the BBC work to strict guidelines in order to prevent legal problems arising from officers claiming they've been portrayed as corrupt on the small screen.

But in the real world of police corruption, there is one notorious squad of detectives who've found themselves at the centre of more controversy than any other unit inside Britain's police forces. Scotland Yard's Flying Squad, as it came to be known, was founded back in 1919 – shortly after the end of the First World War. It was first set up by police inspector Walter Hambrook, who led a team of detectives that had been given special dispensation to arrest criminals anywhere in the Metropolitan Police District.

The twelve-man squad maintained surveillance on the streets from a horse-drawn carriage van, which was actually a canvas-covered Great Western Railway van with spy holes cut in the side. Criminals quickly dubbed them 'the heavy mob', and this hand-picked body of officers were soon handling some of London's most high-profile cases, concentrating mainly on armed robberies.

In those days, London was experiencing a huge crime wave fuelled by large numbers of First World War squaddies recently released from the armed forces. They'd emerged onto the streets of London and other UK cities, many of them hardened to violence after experiencing the carnage of the Western Front.

Hambrook and his squad soon struck fear into the underworld by tracking known criminals, including robbers, housebreakers and pickpockets, and then lifting them off the streets, literally. This 'heavy mob' also regularly went undercover in pubs and clubs, where informants provided information on other criminals. It was the first time the police had officially used criminals in such a way. Inspector Hambrook and his detectives rapidly evolved into a small unit of Branch C1, Central CID, and were known at Scotland Yard as the 'Mobile Patrol Experiment'.

Those early units enjoyed rapid crime-busting success. In 1920, they were provided with two motor tenders capable of a top speed of 35 mph. (The speed limit at the time was just 20 mph.) A *Daily Mail* journalist duly referred to them as 'a flying squad of hand-picked detectives', and the name stuck. The squad's nickname in rhyming slang, 'The Sweeney' (from Flying Squad/Sweeney Todd, the notorious Fleet Street barber who turned his customers into meat pies), has been around so long that it's now generally regarded as a cliché.

The Flying Squad's primary function to this day is to detect and prevent serious professional crimes and the criminals who commit them. They even use specially trained drivers, recruited from the uniformed divisions of London's Metropolitan Police and given the honorary title of Detective Constable while serving in the squad. By 1929, The Sweeney had become a superbly organised London police unit consisting of forty officers led by a C1 Branch Detective Superintendent.

This was without doubt the squad's honeymoon period for by 1938, the nation's police forces were at least 10,000 men under-strength and London was once again being overrun by petty criminals. The Metropolitan Police had just 1,400 detectives out of a force of 20,000 men. However, most public attention was focused more on the so-called glamorous activities of the small elite teams of police officers, especially the Flying Squad.

By the 1950s, postwar criminal legends like Billy Hill and Jack Spot had consolidated their power and influence in London, plus there was the emergence of soon-to-be notorious gangs including the Krays and Richardsons. The activities of these so-called Kings of the Underworld encouraged the Flying Squad to ramp up their activities.

But despite this, back then 'allegations of malpractice' were not taken very seriously. When, in 1955, senior London police superintendent Bert Hannan produced a report on corruption in London's West End Central police station, the then Met commissioner, Sir John Nott-Bower, went to the station, stood on a chair and reassured his troops that he did not believe a word of it.

The squad at that time was led by an eccentric character called Tommy Butler, who considered himself virtually above the law when it came to nailing down the 'bad guys'. If *Line of Duty* creator Jed Mercurio was to come up with a fictional character like Butler, he'd no doubt be told he was not believable. Butler was an unmarried, 24-hours-a-day policeman with little or no interest in anything other than police business. He often worked into the early hours in his office at Scotland Yard, and lived on sandwiches and food from the police canteen. Colleagues later said he resembled an emaciated concentration-camp survivor, and in his twisted mind everyone was a potential criminal – it was only a matter of time before they were all behind bars.

But in truth Butler's respect for justice and fair play was virtually non-existent. Other policeman grew weary of him because of his manic, almost blind single-mindedness. It was this fear of him that prevented Butler rising to a higher rank in the force, not to mention rumours of 'bungs' (bribes) he'd received from some of the capital's most notorious criminals. In order to secure his dream job as overall commander of the Flying Squad, Butler had to be promoted to chief superintendent. But he was never given that title by his superiors, although many acknowledge he was effectively the boss to squad members of all ranks.

These days, Tommy Butler's questionable policing methods would have been easily exposed by contemporary, standard forensic science and the real-life equivalent of *Line of Duty's* AC-12. But back in the 1950s, re-writing criminals' statements and planting 'bent' evidence was regularly used to help convict many supposed criminals. A lot of officers themselves saw nothing wrong with that because they believed it was their 'duty' to convict criminals by 'any means necessary'.

And throughout all this, Butler met underworld informants at any time of the day or night. And it was Butler – the thin-shouldered, uninteresting bank manager lookalike – who was always there at the final arrest. Surprisingly, he even admitted privately that he felt great sympathy for the families of some criminals, who faced extremely long jail sentences as the Establishment tried to hit back at the underworld.

The hard-nosed, knocking-down-doors habits of the Flying Squad naturally made detectives vulnerable to accusations of corruption. Officers were alleged to have either turned a blind eye to what was going on in return for a cut of the action or – if the information led to the recovery of stolen property – pocketing some of the reward money that the detective would claim on an informant's behalf.

Another corrupt 'service' offered was that a strategically placed officer could also – for a fee – ensure bail was granted, hold back evidence and details about past convictions from a court, or pass on to a person under investigation details of a case being made against him. Corrupt cops even sometimes provided warnings about police operations, which would most likely compromise criminals. Crooked officers were even known to frequently hold onto a proportion of whatever valuables they'd recovered during a police inquiry.

One recently retired former detective said: 'Butler and his mates bent the rules any way they wanted and that's where a lot of today's climate of corruption first came from. Most coppers didn't even think they were doing anything wrong half the time.'

Yet in the middle of all this overt corruption, detectives on the Flying Squad were claiming multiple victories in their war with the underworld. They were helped by the fact that security van hold-ups and bank robberies were getting a lot harder to pull off because of so-called new technology, including CCTV cameras.

By the late 1960s, security guards had been introduced to escort large quantities of cash, which meant the robbers had to step up the levels of threats and resort more frequently to violence if they were to continue robbing with ease on the streets of London.

But the spectre of corruption inside the supposedly elite Flying Squad was never far away.

ON THE TAKE

In 1971, the head of the Flying Squad was rotund Commander Ken Drury. His weight problems were no doubt linked to lunches at fancy West End restaurants and dinners at The Savoy. His colleagues said Drury couldn't resist all those tempting gateau trolleys.

And all this was paid for by Britain's leading pornographer, the dapper and urbane Jimmy Humphreys, who had, as they used to say, 'a criminal record as long as your arm'. Humphreys even gave Drury a rowing machine and an exercise bicycle to get the commander fit enough to pick up the fat weekly bribes he was receiving for turning a blind eye to all of Humphreys' illegal activities in Soho. This was 1970s London, after all, when bent police officers felt entitled to all the dancing girls and used fivers that the criminal world could throw at them, in complete contrast to today's much more secretive forms of police dishonesty.

Pornography was one major source of revenue in those days – for both criminals and police. It was a grey area of illegality still waiting for the 'permissive society' to ease restrictive laws. Crooked Jimmy Humphreys was nicknamed 'the Emperor of porn' and 'the Caesar of Soho' by the mass circulation newspapers all based in nearby Fleet Street. Humphreys and his attractive and vivacious wife, Rusty – a former stripper from Kent, whose ambitious mum had once hoped she would become Britain's answer to Shirley Temple – had built up their porn empire after opening a handful of Soho clubs. Humphreys also had nine criminal convictions to his name, one of which had resulted in a spell in the isolated Dartmoor Prison.

Humphreys knew from the moment he arrived in Soho that if he wanted his criminal enterprises to thrive, he'd have to buy police officers 'a drink' on a regular basis: 'a drink' meant anything from a tenner for a so-called 'bobby on the beat' to a couple of grand a month for senior officers like Commander Drury. Whenever police were about to raid one of Humphreys' bookshops, he'd receive a phone call beforehand, often with the advice 'Be like WH Smith' – i.e. get rid of all but a couple of porn books.

Jimmy Humphreys had originally learned the ropes from his mentor, Bernie Silver, a previous 'emperor of Soho', who'd made a fortune from brothels and strip joints. Silver told Humphreys the golden rule with detectives was: 'Get 'em young'. That way you could rely on them as they moved up the promotion ladder. Humphreys even made sure the wives of his corrupt cops were also looked after. On one occasion, a detective returned Humphreys' gift of a necklace because his wife's neck was too thick for it and he wanted a larger one.

When Flying Squad commander Ken Drury's connection to Humphreys was first publicly exposed by a tabloid newspaper, he was served with disciplinary papers and suspended from duty. Drury immediately resigned rather than face a full disciplinary hearing. But before doing so, he wrote an article for the *News of the World,* insisting Humphreys had been one of his informants.

The notorious pornographer was furious. He was worried about the ways in which these allegations would affect his relationships with numerous underworld associates, including other crooked police officers. There was even a risk that other criminals might come after him now he'd been branded 'a grass' by Drury.

So, a week later, Humphreys got his revenge by giving an interview to the same newspaper which had run Drury's claims. Humphreys said he'd never received any money from Drury and in fact he'd wined and dined the police chief on a total of fifty-eight occasions, during which Humphreys always picked up the bill. Flying Squad chief Ken Drury had been caught bang to rights, as they say in the underworld.

But Drury – like so many corrupt cops portrayed in *Line of Duty* – wouldn't give up without a fight. He was so deluded, he didn't even consider himself 'bent'. Drury insisted it was 'absolutely essential' for Flying Squad officers to mix socially with people connected with the criminal fraternity. In other words, he saw all those lunches as being a legitimate part of his job.

It then emerged that Ken Drury had felt 'relaxed enough' to take a holiday in Cyprus with Humphreys and his wife Rusty. Drury's slippery slope ended with a dawn raid by his colleagues, who escorted him from his home with a blanket over his head.

A 1977 Old Bailey trial resulted in an eight-year jail sentence and a lot more front-page tabloid headlines.

CLIMATE OF CORRUPTION

The problem with Ken Drury's philosophy was that it blatantly enabled criminals to manipulate detectives. Criminals would (and still do) happily help police in an effort to divert attention from their own activities while at the same time obtaining, through the usefulness of the information given, a degree of protection from prosecution.

In 1970s London, criminals were even regularly collecting cash rewards for pointing the police in the right direction. This often enabled them to get their rivals taken off the streets so they could further pursue all their illegal activities unhindered.

In 1973, Detective Chief Superintendent Albert Wickstead – aka 'The Grey Fox' – head of the Yard's Serious Crimes Squad, came up with a classic diversionary tactic. He ordered the Flying Squad to carry out multiple high-profile raids by 235 officers, which resulted in 93 men and 1 woman being hauled into custody. One senior detective told the *Daily Express* at the time: 'The other side have never been hit so hard.'

But many flying squad officers later told me that the raids were nothing more than a publicity stunt to try and water down all the damage caused by the Drury police corruption revelations. After being asked a few awkward questions by politicians and the media, Scotland Yard then assistant commissioner Gilbert Kelland – a supposedly straight-arrow officer leading Scotland Yard's operation against corruption, – wrote: 'We strongly believed that, for the eventual benefit of the force, the crow of corruption had to be nailed to the barn door to convince and remind everyone of the need for positive action and eternal vigilance.'

Indeed.

BETRAYAL

So, during the 1970s, an ever-expanding cloud of dark corruption was looming over Scotland Yard – and not just the Flying Squad.

After a *Sunday Times* exposé, three corrupt members of the drugs squad found themselves in the dock in front of Mr Justice Melford Stevenson, who sent them down and delivered a famous sentencing speech: 'You poisoned the wells of criminal justice and set about it deliberately. What is equally bad is that you have betrayed your comrades in the Metropolitan Police Force which enjoys the respect of the civilised world – what remains of it – and not the least grave aspect of what you have done is provide material for the crooks, cranks and do-gooders who unite to attack the police whenever the opportunity arises.'

One notorious veteran bank robber, Bobby King, later recalled: 'I can't remember one local CID officer who wasn't crooked back in those days.' King and many of his criminal associates believed every problem could be solved with a bribe. It costs £25 to continue driving while disqualified; £2,000 to wriggle out of a police assault charge. This included the officer explaining his own injuries to a magistrate – 'I could have fallen in the scuffle'. Possession of firearm charges would be dropped for a few hundred pounds. The accepted etiquette was that, on being arrested, a professional criminal would ask the detective if 'something could be done'.

Charlie Richardson – the notorious south London gang leader who ended up getting twenty-five years at the Old Bailey for violence, fraud and extortion – said in his autobiography, *My Manor*: 'The most lucrative, powerful and extensive protection racket ever to exist was administered by the Metropolitan Police. It was a sort of taxation on crime... sometimes we would pay people to be "found" committing small crimes so that our friendly local protection racketeer in blue could have someone to arrest and look like he had been busy.'

Richardson was correct, of course. There were bad cops lurking in all four corners of Scotland Yard. A classic example was Detective Chief Superintendent Bill Moody, head of the Obscene Publications Squad, or the 'Dirty Squad' as it was presciently known at the time. He drove a Lancia and was on the payroll of both the Met and Flying Squad commander Ken Drury's friend Jimmy Humphreys.

Moody's nickname was 'Wicked Bill'. He and his boss, the debonair commander Wally Virgo – one of the top detectives at the Yard – pocketed £53,000 between them in bribes over the course of sixteen months. No small sum in the early seventies. Virgo and Moody were eventually jailed for twelve years each, although Virgo was released on appeal and died a few years later.

Peter Scott – one of Britain's most prolific cat burglars and the subject of the 1965 film *He Who Rides a Tiger* – knew Wally Virgo well. Scott later recalled: 'Poor Wally. He was basically a straight-hand, but when he saw that everyone else was in the pot, greed got the better of him. I felt a bit sorry for him. In those days the wages for the police weren't that good and there was no fat pension to look forward to, like there is now, so for someone like Wally to get £500 a month or whatever it was – it was just too tempting. I saw him after he was convicted. He couldn't look me in the eye – he'd reduced himself to my level.'

Jury nobbling and interference with star witnesses had become virtually a weekly occurrence at London's big courts, including the Old Bailey during this period. None of it would have been able to thrive without wholesale police corruption. The Director of Public Prosecutions regularly objected to bail applications by villains on the basis that there was a 'strong fear' of interference by witnesses. But then they'd be allowed their freedom, thanks to 'a word in the right ear'.

One of the few white knights on the horizon at this time was then Metropolitan Police Commissioner Sir Robert Mark, who tried his hardest to clean up the Yard. He upset many of his senior colleagues by publicly describing the Yard's detective units as 'the most routinely corrupt organisation in London'.

The old music-hall song 'If You Want to Know the Time, Ask a Policeman' was based on a belief prevalent at the time that officers stole the watches off drunken toffs.

Initially, Mark encountered enormous resistance in his

efforts to purge the Yard of corruption. Many officers from those days well remember his classic statement that 'a good police force arrests more criminals than it employs'. During Mark's commissionership, 50 officers were prosecuted and 478 left early. But this was nothing more than scratching the surface, for back inside the notorious Flying Squad, corruption was still rampant.

Detectives were being put under so much pressure to increase the number of arrests that they were actively trying to persuade members of close-knit gangs to inform on robberies in advance. This new directive would inevitably lead to even more police corruption.

SUPERGRASSES

Flying Squad detectives were ordered to turn even more hardened criminals into police informants. These villains would soon be dubbed 'supergrasses'. However, their notoriety would eventually prove a springboard for the exposure of corrupt officers across Scotland Yard.

The most notorious of all supergrass cases was the controversial so-called chit-to-freedom bank robber Bertie Smalls, negotiated from the Flying Squad in the early 1970s. Smalls' decision to 'join the other side' turned him into one of the most hated men in the London underworld. Many villains pledged revenge. One bank robber later told me he'd have 'gladly killed that bastard for nothing. He was vermin and should have been wiped off the face of this earth.'

It seemed that the Flying Squad had become so obsessed

with catching robbers preying on security vans that they were prepared to bend the rules outrageously in order to win their war with professional criminals. At this time the Flying Squad regularly hauled in up-and-coming villains suspected of being connected to particular crimes. But they had no way of actually proving it. So these criminals were then offered immunity if they informed on their associates.

However, this created such a climate of hatred between the police and the underworld that crime bosses began trying to frame high-ranking police officers in order to cut the number of supergrass cases. The crime bosses' primary aim was to smear the names of officers so badly that their evidence would be thrown out of court during high-profile criminal trials. And sometimes it worked.

It also further fuelled corrupt relationships between detectives and criminals.

It took some years before senior officers at Scotland Yard realised that the Flying Squad was spending more of its time chasing criminals who might be prepared to pay them bribes than catching villains in the act of committing crimes. So, eventually, Sweeney detectives were ordered to pull back from dealing with most informants, who were helping fuel most of the corruption problems in the first place.

Instead, these so-called elite thief-takers were simply sent out onto the streets of London to look for robbers on the traditional workers' payday of Thursday. To many observers it looked like a desperate measure. 'It was ludicrous when I look back on it, but we had little choice in the matter,' explained one retired Flying Squad officer.

Some detectives, however, secretly nurtured criminals just as before and offered to 'help them out' in exchange for inside information that might help those officers to catch other criminals in action. It seemed as if most of the top brass at Scotland Yard remained in complete denial that corruption even existed on a big scale.

THE 'NEW' FLYING SQUAD

Eventually, Scotland Yard publicly pledged to completely overhaul the Flying Squad. Detectives formed a central robbery squad, which would be run from a co-ordinating unit at Scotland Yard, with four smaller groups strategically located around London.

Typically, senior officers insisted this was more to do with old-fashioned thief-taking than corruption by telling the underworld loud and clear: 'We're out to get you.' Even after crooked Commander Ken Drury's exposure, the top brass still couldn't bring themselves to concede that corruption was ongoing and deeply problematic.

For many old-school criminals, the Flying Squad's corruption problems were further evidence that their old enemy occupied the same moral ground as the very people they were supposed to be bringing to justice. Few in the underworld believed that the Flying Squad would suddenly become honourable and honest overnight.

Former robber Eric Mason later explained: 'People began to realise that anything was fair game. The Establishment had been caught out. People knew that politicians, people we looked up to, were just as bent as the police, and people lost respect. People began to realise it was all a big con.'

This climate of corruption was clearly here to stay.

TURNING THE OTHER CHEEK

By the late 1970s, the image of Scotland Yard's Flying Squad was taking quite a battering. Some detectives were being viewed with as much suspicion as the criminals they dealt with. There were even rumours that some of London's supposedly finest detectives had developed cocaine habits, fed by some of the drugs they'd confiscated while pursuing criminals.

And throughout this period, old-time professional criminals continued to look on the police – and in particular, the Flying Squad – as the 'enemy'. Sometimes criminals would appear to be helping the police in order to divert attention from their own activities and ensure a degree of protection from prosecution.

It seemed that some detectives back then were still either turning a blind eye to what was going on in return for a cut of the action or – if the information led to the recovery of stolen property – pocketing some of the reward money that the detectives would claim on the informant's behalf. Corrupt officers also held onto a proportion of whatever valuables they recovered during an inquiry.

And for a fee, officers continued to ensure bail was granted, hold back evidence and details about past convictions from a court, or pass on to a person under investigation details of a case being made against him. They were also given warnings in advance about police operations in which they could be compromised.

The police were even accused of providing criminals with warnings about covert operations. These offences usually revolved around investigations of crimes such as bank robberies, drugs and obscene publications. Some officers actually believed the system of justice was weighted against them, so they felt justified in bending the rules.

Clearly, nothing had changed.

SHOOT TO KILL

In the 1980s, the Flying Squad unofficially issued a chilling message to the robbers of London: *You'll be shot dead if you carry arms.* To some criminals at that time, the police had turned themselves into judge, jury and executioner all rolled into one. In fact, all it really did was stiffen the underworld's resolve to beat the police by whatever means and it helped re-emphasise the importance of corrupt police officers when it came to London's professional criminals.

As one former Flying Squad detective later explained: 'Issuing a shoot-to-kill warning to armed robbers was a very risky strategy and many officers thought it was a red herring to try and take people's attention away from all the corruption problems.'

Another retired detective told me: 'A lot of these robbers had their own tame corrupt officers working on their behalf inside the Flying Squad, so the last thing they wanted was to send their paymasters to an early grave.'

One former Flying Squad detective recently told me he was a member of that unofficial unit of officers who patrolled London and were prepared to carry out the 'shoot to kill' policy when it came to armed robbers on the streets of the capital. As he said: 'Yeah, I don't deny being part of that armed shoot-to-kill unit, but robbers were making the streets dangerous for law abiding citizens back then, so they needed to be dealt with. We were fighting a losing battle and we were determined to take those streets back from the villains. So if push came to shove, we knew we'd have to shoot any robbers who posed a threat to us or the public.'

Numerous retired police officers believe the shoot-to-kill policy helped fuel further police corruption because it made the police themselves much more powerful. After all, they had – in effect – been sanctioned to carry out state-sponsored executions.

In July 1987, professional criminals Michael Flynn and Nicholas Payne were shot dead by police during an attempted robbery of a wages van at an abattoir in Shooters Hill, south London. In November 1987, robber Tony Ash was shot dead during a wages snatch at a Bejam supermarket in Woolwich, south-east London. A TV crew was even on hand, to ensure a very public execution.

Many robbers who survived these shootings later insisted there had been no warnings issued by the Flying Squad that they were going to fire.

One former Sweeney detective recently told me: 'We had to do something. The old-school gangs were running rings round us. They was putting two fingers up at us and saying "come and get us". As for this policy encouraging corruption, bent coppers had been around since Victorian days. Killing a few villains didn't suddenly make us all bent though.'

It seemed to many at this time as though the Flying Squad – now relocated to Limehouse police station, in the heart of the East End – were single-mindedly trying to rip London's robbery gangs to shreds. It would eventually lead to cat-and-mouse games over the following two decades, peppered with accusations ranging from bribery to the alleged participation of police detectives in actual robberies.

Some officers remain convinced to this day that the success of the Flying Squad at that time was mainly down to 'playing the game'. One former detective explained: 'I have no doubt that we got the steer on countless robberies in advance because we allowed ourselves to be manipulated by criminals who wanted to get their rivals and enemies off the streets. They wanted us to shoot those robbers dead. We were doing their dirty work for them, in a sense.'

And not even high-powered inquiries run by independent police officers from outside forces were able to put a lid on the corrupt activities of certain officers at Scotland Yard.

Around this time, Scotland Yard Commissioner Sir Paul Condon told a House of Commons select committee that there were still hundreds of crooked cops operating inside London's police. 'I honestly believe I command the most honourable large city police service in the world,' he said. 'However, I do have a minority of officers who are corrupt, dishonest, unethical… They commit crimes, they neutralise evidence in important cases and they betray police operations and techniques to criminals... they are very difficult to target and prosecute.'

As a result, there was a huge recruitment problem when it came to providing officers for newly formed anti-corruption units. This was something that AC-12 chief Ted Hastings faced in *Line of Duty*'s first episode and it's been a recurring theme throughout the five series of the show.

One former Flying Squad detective elaborated: 'Detectives were reluctant to join an anti-corruption unit because it wasn't seen as the right thing to do. On the contrary, it was regarded as a betrayal. Also, it was believed that a lot of uniformed officers had applied, which made many of us think that uniform would be out to "get us all", the allegedly bent detectives. No decent detective would want to be part of that.'

Former detective superintendent Graham Satchwell – himself investigated and cleared by several internal Scotland Yard inquiries – admitted that a lot of 'results-driven' detectives considered internal investigation officers as – at best – 'a nuisance'. Satchwell – author of the memoir, *An Inspector Recalls* – said that 'the abiding memory of those who investigated me is of incompetence and stupidity. Those who run internal complaints departments are always close to the most senior ranks, so whatever they do is authorised. Invariably now, such work attracts ambitious officers.'

Today, endemic police corruption is often blamed by many officers on the police's reluctance to react all those years earlier when those warning signs first appeared on the horizon. Meanwhile, bribery and corruption continued to colour most old-school criminals' attitude towards the police. Their argument was simple: 'How can you trust a copper if most of them want a backhander? They're the enemy, but most of them are less honest than we are.'

So the immense cancer of corruption continued to grow inside the Metropolitan Police and by all accounts many other UK police forces. Many professional criminals believed everything could still be bought from the police for a price.

A lot of villains insisted on using a middleman – often a figure well known to the police – to hand over bribes. As usual, many officers insisted these claims were just smears by known criminals on hard-working detectives. But as one old-time bank robber later recalled: 'There was hundreds of ways to bribe a copper and that was part and parcel of your business and you accepted that. You even built it into your finances.'

And then there was the practice of 'verballing' – police inserting words into a suspect's statement – which many professional criminals claimed continued to be used against them to secure arrests. This involved the police fabricating a statement, which immediately inferred the suspect had committed a crime because of his use of certain words. One notorious robber later told me: 'Once the cozzers had our names as suspects from a grass, we knew we was in trouble because they'd falsify the evidence, then arrest us and secure convictions.'

Most honest detectives simply shrugged their shoulders when corrupt practices were discussed openly between officers. There was a feeling of complete and utter apathy when it came to such subjects.

In London and the south-east of England there were more sophisticated gangs of corrupt officers. Not only were they working inside supposedly elite units such as the Flying Squad, but also inside regional crime squads.

In south London, a gang of renegade officers even had close connections to many of the criminals planning one of the biggest heists of the last century. It was a pivotal, headline-hitting crime, one that would eventually unravel a spider's web of UK police corruption on a level never seen before.

THE BIG ONE

On Saturday, 26 November 1983, an armed gang carried out Britain's largest ever gold-bullion robbery at a commercial building near London's Heathrow Airport.

More than £25 million worth of gold bars (worth £500 million today) bound for the Far East were stolen from the Brink's-Mat warehouse, about a mile outside the airport perimeter, between 6.30 am and 8.15 am.

A gang of at least six men – all armed and wearing balaclavas – overcame the guards and handcuffed them. One was hit on the head with a pistol and two had petrol poured over them. Then the robbers successfully disabled a huge array of electronic security devices. They even used the warehouse's own forklift trucks to transport the 76 boxes of gold bars into a waiting van.

Insurers offered a reward of £2 million for information leading to the recovery of the 6,800 gold bars – which were all identifiable by refiners' stamps.

The Brink's-Mat gang had expected rich pickings, but they'd never imagined the extraordinary level of potential wealth they stumbled upon that day. Their audacious plot, ruthless in its conception and brilliant in its execution, had just landed them the biggest haul of gold in British criminal history. Brink's-Mat would go on to make the names and fortunes of many of the UK's most notorious gangsters and there was plenty of money on offer from the gang to corrupt police officers.

Commander Frank Cater was Scotland Yard's Flying Squad boss at that time. He led the hunt for the thieves, but the spectre of police corruption hung over this heist within hours of the robbery being committed. For this robbery's bloody tentacles sparked a vicious, deadly gang war in the underworld that cost police officers and criminals their lives.

Many of the professional criminals involved had their own 'tame' coppers. And those corrupt officers soon found themselves being dragged into the deadly fallout from the heist. As one former detective who served on the inquiry later explained: 'These were old-school professional villains and they expected their bent coppers to help them beat the charges they faced and keep them one step ahead of the police's robbery investigation team.'

But how and why did all this police corruption begin? Why were these once honest officers drawn to such a high-risk crime? To try and find the answers one must first delve right back into the parallel history of the south-east London underworld, where so many of the police officers grew up alongside those who would become professional criminals.

It's also the same 'manor' of London where the *Line of Duty*'s Steve Arnott is supposed to have been brought up.

Back in the 1980s, the relationship between the police and professional criminals had become one based to a certain degree on mutual respect. Often they'd meet each other in the local pub and exchange pleasantries, even though they might have been 'nicked' by that same officer the previous week. Many police officers involved in the Brink's-Mat investigation had grown up alongside the men who'd pulled off the heist and other infamous robberies at that time. They'd even come from the same neighbourhoods and some even went to school together.

In fact, the Brink's-Mat gang themselves had had connections with officers in both the Kent force and the Met since long before they pulled off the actual heist. Some of the robbers had even been invited to CID functions and parties held inside police stations in south London and Kent. But following the heist, many honest officers who knew of the gang members initially tried to step back from the investigation, fearful they might be 'smeared' by the robbers and their associates.

When three of the suspected robbers were arrested soon after the robbery on purely circumstantial evidence, they all refused to sign the police's contemporaneous notes of their interviews. They were convinced the police would frame them, even if they managed to get their own 'tame' officers to intervene. The suspects – all well-known old-school professional criminals – knew that the veracity of such unsigned statements could therefore be questioned by their lawyers in court. Any mistakes they may have made, any slips that opened up a chink in their armour, could be dismissed as fabrication. Without signatures at the bottom of each page, all the records taken could be labelled as 'verbals'. That meant a prisoner's statement could have been fabricated by officers in order to guarantee their guilt.

The Brink's-Mat heist itself also marked the appearance of two ruthless young gangsters, who'd been brought in to help smelt the vast amount of stolen gold bullion. They were already well known in south-east London, the West Country and Kent. Both claimed to have numerous crooked contacts. Not only bent coppers but also corrupt judges. They even boasted of 'owning' some MPs in London and Birmingham. One of these gangsters even deliberately befriended a secretary at a police station in south-east England. He persuaded the woman to meet for a drink after work one night. They began an affair and she provided him with information about how the Brink's-Mat investigation was progressing. When the gangster discovered he was sharing the woman's affections with a senior detective that made the affair even more exciting and 'productive'.

Out and about at their favourite pubs in south-east London and Kent, the members of the Brink's-Mat gang who hadn't been arrested also tried to gauge the intensity of the police investigation through certain second-division criminals, many of whom also had other contacts in the police.

'The key to the Brink's-Mat investigation were the corrupt senior police officers who knew most of the gang,' one recently retired south London detective explained. 'This gave the criminals access to certain information virtually from the moment the crime was committed.' Police even discovered that the Brink's-Mat robbers had obtained all the arms they used on the heist from a former corrupt police officer, who'd set himself up as an illegal arms dealer after being earlier dismissed from the police.

When one gang member was arrested, he immediately named a senior Scotland Yard detective as someone who'd vouch for him. There was no doubt these gangsters had friends in high places. That same senior police officer never talked openly about his relationship with any of the criminals connected to the Brink's-Mat robbery. But other officers who worked with this officer knew all about his link to the criminals. One former south London detective later recalled: 'Half of us thought this copper was a terrific asset and the other half thought he was bent as arseholes and taking us to the cleaners.'

At Kent's Dartford police station – following the first interview of one suspect after he'd been arrested – a short statement was drawn up of what the suspect had said. He requested that the letters 'p.m.' be inserted after the time 'one o'clock'. The suspect then asked that a line be drawn from the end of the last word on each line to the edge of the page to prevent anything being inserted later by rogue police officers. It seems even this powerful gangster feared he could be stitched up by crooked cops beyond his control. He was convinced his underworld enemies were determined to get him imprisoned, so they could swoop in and steal the gold bullion.

So-called straight detectives working on the Brink's-Mat inquiry were not at all surprised to discover that many of their colleagues were allegedly in the pockets of these hardened old-time professional criminals, and by this time, senior officers at Scotland Yard were already feeling embarrassed by some of the corrupt cop allegations swirling around the Brink's-Mat robbery. As a result, the Flying Squad were unofficially ordered to crack down even harder on other gangs of robbers. The aim was to water down the allegations surrounding the raid, which were threatening to seriously impact on the public's trust of the police at that time.

SMOKESCREEN

Meanwhile, in the badlands of south London, rumours were circulating that some Brink's-Mat suspects were so close to certain detectives that the charges against them would soon be thrown out. One former Kent detective later recalled: 'I heard that once a few bob had been thrown in the right direction, some gang members would at least get bail and freedom, despite the serious nature of their alleged crimes.'

One member of the gang was so confident he could bribe his way out of trouble that he allowed the police to hold an identity parade that he believed would be faked, so he could then be released. However, the parade was cancelled at the last minute when senior officers received information that it was indeed going to be faked.

Then associates of the gang spread rumours that some of the men had been arrested over another robbery some time before Brink's-Mat and that officers had falsified their statements for that crime. This was a deliberate smokescreen to help 'muddy the waters' so that anti-corruption investigators were unable to pin any suspected officers down.

Meanwhile, straight Brink's-Mat detectives tried to keep tabs on what was happening to avoid being implicated in any corrupt practices. This then further encouraged some rogue officers to nurture their favourite villains in the hope they could continue to 'earn a few bob'. Eventually, some honest detectives began putting pressure on the Brink's-Mat robbery suspects in custody to name corrupt cops to investigators. But as one of them later told me: 'Why the fuck would I want to help the cozzers catch one of their own? I told 'em to fuck off.'

At Albany Prison on the Isle of White, a detective visited one Brink's-Mat gangster three times to try and persuade him to help their investigations into one particular allegedly corrupt senior Scotland Yard officer. The detective in question owned a half-million pound house (worth £4 million in today's property market) on the outskirts of London and a villa abroad. He was very well known to most members of the Brink's-Mat gang. The same officer had even been the subject of a full-scale inquiry by Metropolitan Police Commissioner Robert Mark's anti-police corruption creation, A10.

The investigation – under the supervision of the independent Police Complaints Authority – was secretly launched when a detective constable arrested a drug dealer in south-east London, who made allegations against various officers including this particular detective. The investigation centred on the senior officer's relationships with his informants – one of whom allegedly was a member of the Brink's-Mat gang. The same officer refused to co-operate with the internal investigation, saying there was no way he'd help the 'opposition'. With no tangible evidence, the investigation against that detective was dropped.

The failure to prosecute certain gangsters clearly linked to the Brink's-Mat heist also seemed to imply that they had friends in high places. However, this was never substantiated. But there is no doubt that crooked police officers, dodgy lawyers and property developers, as well as gun-runners and drug-traffickers in the UK, Spain and the US, were all involved with the Brink's-Mat gang in the months and years following the heist.

Profits from the robbery continued to be laundered and then invested in areas including the London Docklands development, where they would yield extraordinary dividends. At least 50 per cent of the land that would be developed into the financial community of Canary Wharf in the late 1980s and early 1990s was purchased in the eighties with money from the Brink's-Mat robbery. One former robber later told me: 'Naturally, the lads had put some more cash aside to keep bribing the cozzers to also make sure they kept other villains away from their stashes of cash and gold from the Brink's-Mat job.'

The heist had not only changed the face of police corruption in the south-east of England, it also turned the screws on some extremely vulnerable characters.

PUSHED TO THE LIMIT

In series one of *Line of Duty*, crooked police detective Gates (played by Lennie James) commits suicide rather than face his accusers.

The shame of police corruption in the real world can also sometimes push an officer into an abyss of hopelessness. 'It can even be seen as an easy way out. Not only for the officer in question but his other corrupt colleagues as well,' explained one former Flying Squad detective. 'Taking your own life is obviously not the answer. Abandoning your family and your colleagues in that way is a tragic waste.'

Another retired officer said: 'Some crooked cops never think about what will happen when they're caught until it's too late. A lot of them have plunged into corruption through desperation, whether it be a shortage of cash or an addiction to drugs or gambling. Then they get busted and it finally dawns on them that they've deceived everyone in their life who cares about them. It's a hard cross to bear.'

When Gates kills himself at the end of series one, many in the audience were unsympathetic. But real detectives say the pressure of the job can be so intense that it's surprising not more have taken their lives. One of the most tragic real-life examples of this came – as with so much when it comes to UK police corruption – during the bloody aftermath of the Brink's-Mat gold bullion robbery, back in the mid-1980s.

Detective Constable Alan 'Taffy' Holmes was a member of Scotland Yard's Serious Crime Squad and one of the chief investigators probing the Brink's-Mat gold bullion heist.

Yet in July 1987, Holmes shot himself dead in the garden of his Croydon, Surrey, home. He'd apparently 'cracked' after being questioned for hours by officers from Scotland Yard's Complaints Investigation Bureau about his association with certain criminals and a senior serving officer, who was rumoured to be corrupt.

No one knows to this day exactly why Taffy Holmes took his own life, but the spectre of corruption did loom over him and it seemed to send him spiralling towards his own premature death. Today, Taffy Holmes's onetime colleagues feel very conflicted about his death. One retired south London detective recalled: 'Taffy was a lovely fella. Sure, he skated on thin ice a bit, but then so did many of us back then. But he had a very sensitive side. He could be got at and a number of officers steamed into him when there was speculation that he was too close to one specific gang boss.'

At that time, this same criminal was one of the police's most hated figures following the death of an undercover police officer, who'd been working on surveillance of that same gangster's home. The criminal was eventually acquitted of the murder when the jury accepted that he'd used self-defence when he found 'a stranger' in his garden. However, certain detectives were outraged at the acquittal and prioritised 'getting' the crime boss. This meant exposing all his relationships with police officers, including, allegedly, Taffy Holmes's. It became clear to senior police officers that the crime boss had a 'stable' of corrupt police officers on his books.

As Taffy Holmes's onetime colleague later explained: 'That

same criminal collected coppers like other people collect stamps but that didn't mean they were all corrupt. But Taffy must have thought he was on a hiding to nothing and certain senior officers wanted his head on a plate.'

Holmes was put under police surveillance initially. It's never been revealed if there was any concrete evidence of corruption against him. 'But he knew he was going to be given the chop – retired early – at the very least and being a copper was his life. He didn't want to leave The Job,' added Holmes's former colleague.

Meanwhile, crimes linking corrupt police officers to the Brink's-Mat robbery continued. A few months after Taffy Holmes's death, one of the police's most chilling corruption-linked murders was allegedly committed. Again, it left a trail that snaked all the way back to the Brink's-Mat heist.

DANIEL MORGAN

Line of Duty's prolific scriptwriters have created some pretty outrageous storylines through the programme's five series to date. But they all pale into insignificance compared to the real-life murder of private eye Daniel Morgan.

In November 1987, he was found with an axe embedded in his skull in a south-east London car park. Detectives involved in the inquiry believed Morgan had been killed because he was about to expose police corruption linked to the Brink's-Mat robbery. It was rumoured that Morgan had a gang of money launderers under surveillance, who had close connections to crooked police officers in the south-east of England.

Two former detectives were eventually acquitted of all illicit activities in connection with Daniel Morgan's murder and the case remains unsolved to this day.

One of my oldest criminal contacts in that area of London later told me: 'That guy Morgan got caught right in the middle of a fire fight between corrupt cozzers and a bunch of nasty gangsters. All of them got paranoid they were about to be turned over by Morgan, who'd actually stumbled into their activities while on another investigation. You could say he was in the wrong place at the wrong time.'

Reverberations from the murder of Daniel Morgan have rumbled on for more than thirty years. It is seen by many police officers as the ultimate example of how renegade police officers turned into deadly criminals. But as one retired detective later explained: 'Morgan's murder was the tip of the iceberg. Back then, probably 30 per cent of all coppers in south London and Kent were suspected of being on the take. This culture of corruption had become an everyday fact of life.

'A lot of us thought that the murder of an innocent man [Morgan] would spell the downfall of many of those bent coppers, but nothing could be further from the truth. The bosses at the Yard never properly investigated the killing and there has been a perception ever since that a bunch of bad cops got away with it.'

Back on that same manor of south-east London, rumours continued to sweep the underworld that Morgan had been killed by serving police officers on the orders of their gangland associates. The officers in question were alleged to be close to a south London criminal, who later helped bring another crooked policeman to justice. And once again the name of one particular officer was mentioned in connection with Mr Morgan's murder. This was the same officer, mentioned in connection with the Brink's-Mat robbery, who lived in a detached mansion on the outskirts of London and also owned a villa abroad. He had connections with the most powerful criminals in the south London and Kent underworld and had even been the subject of a full-scale inquiry by the Yard's Complaints Investigations Bureau. But he was never named in public.

On the streets of south-east London and in police stations across the capital and Kent, many were watching with nervous interest as murder, double-dealing corrupt cops and betrayal continued to engulf increasing numbers of those associated with the Brink's-Mat robbery.

It's highly likely the murder of Daniel Morgan inspired *Line of Duty* creator Jed Mercurio, especially as it occurred right in the heart of south-east London where his fictional AC-12 hero Steve Arnott had been born and bred.

Mercurio is a master at creating fascinating, intricate characters, as he did for *Line of Duty's* three main roles. Their backgrounds contain significant clues about how police corruption in the real world evolves and these officers are the lifeblood of the show.

Chapter Two

STAYING IN CHARACTER

'I was tempted. No one had seen that stash of cash except me. I looked around and stuffed it in my pocket. Now I was a bent copper, too.'

Corrupt officer on temptation

STEVE ARNOTT

Examining in depth the characters of the three main anti-corruption officers at the centre of TV's *Line of Duty* provides a fascinating insight into the state of real-life modern-day police corruption.

Line of Duty detective Steve Arnott speaks with a distinct south-east London accent in the series, even though actor Martin Compston is actually Scottish born and bred. Arnott's south-east London connections are a crucial part of his backstory in the show. And in real life, the area where he comes from has been a hotbed for professional criminals for more than sixty years. It's also been home to more police corruption than probably anywhere else in the UK.

Many real police and criminals from these parts believe Arnott's background is significant because being brought up in such a notoriously lawless corner of London would make him especially aware of corrupt cops and criminality in general. 'It's a wild place. Things happen here that you don't want to know about,' explained one former south-east London detective.

Most members of 1963's historic Great Train Robbery gang came from the area, as did the majority of professional bank and security van robbers who ruled the streets of London from the 1960s to the early 1990s. It's likely that Arnott's own relatives would have been on both sides of the law, since people with these types of backgrounds have been commonplace in this area of London for many decades.

As another recently retired detective from this part of the city explained: 'This manor has been a hotbed of criminality for as long as anyone can remember. I was a copper from this area, just like Arnott. You often went to school with guys who later became major criminals. There was a bit of respect between us but that would have been a long time before Arnott was even born. There is this tough, no-nonsense mentality that's often passed down in south-east London, whatever side of the law you're on. No wonder he's a tough bastard.'

Another former police officer who watches *Line of Duty* elaborated on this: 'Arnott being from south-east London makes him an even more intriguing character. He's extremely streetwise and seems to know all about that thin line which exists between honesty and corruption. What I like about him even more is that he uses all that background experience to get to the heart of an investigation like all good coppers do.

'No wonder Arnott is a perfect fit for his role in the AC-12 anti-corruption unit. He knows how bent coppers think. He's also artful and sharp; two things you have to be if you're going to bring down bent coppers.'

When Steve Arnott attended Hendon Police Training College, he would no doubt have met other young officers with connections to his old childhood friends from south-east London. As another former detective pointed out: 'This area is a world within an underworld. If you're born and bred in these parts you end up either being a villain or a cop. Arnott would be well aware of this and it would make him doubly alert to any form of criminality. You could say it's in his blood.'

Many aspects of south-east London life have changed in recent years, thanks to vast redevelopment projects and a huge influx of hard-working immigrants pushing many of the so-called baby boomer families out to the suburbs and even further into deepest Kent.

Now in his mid-thirties, Steve Arnott would have originally joined the force about fifteen or sixteen years ago. This is probably too late to have encountered most of the area's most infamous professional criminals, who lived on his home turf in the bad old days. Many of them would have moved out of the region before Arnott even reached adolescence. But no doubt he would have heard all about at least some of them from his own family and childhood friends.

Being surrounded with so much overt criminality would have made Arnott even more determined not to fall into a life of crime. Some fans of the show are convinced that Arnott's own father may well have been one of those very same professional criminals synonymous with south-east London. If that's the case, then one side of Arnott's family would have been appalled by his decision to become a 'cozzer', as they call the police in these parts.

Nevertheless, all this would surely have made him doubly determined not to get involved in any corrupt activities? He knows that behind his back many of his family members and old-school mates would think it was inevitable he'd end up 'bent' like some police officers that originated from this area.

This determination to 'do the right thing' would also explain why Arnott so steadfastly refused to cover up his accidental killing of an innocent man during an armed raid, which led to Arnott's eventual transfer to AC-12 in episode one of series one of *Line of Duty*.

Also typical of the area is the way Arnott's character can sometimes be shifty when it comes to certain subjects. This can wrongly give the show's audience the impression he is guilty of something illicit when that is most certainly not the case.

In series three of *Line of Duty*, Arnott is accused of killing the creepy, psychopathic Detective Inspector Lindsay Denton and then covering up the murder. Some of Arnott's colleagues clearly believed he was guilty and his angry response to being framed didn't help explain his innocence either.

'A lot of people from south-east London sound aggressive

but that doesn't make them guilty,' said one recently retired detective from the same 'manor'. 'Round these parts you don't stop to ask the time, you don't look people in the eyes either. It's a dog-eat-dog sort of environment and Arnott knows that only too well.'

No wonder there's an inner steeliness to Steve Arnott. 'People round here don't back down easily, which is why they make such successful criminals *and* police officers,' added the same former detective.

That inner resilience shines through Arnott's character when he's almost killed after being thrown down a set of stairs in series four by a murder suspect. Arnott ends up in a wheelchair, with doctors giving him only a slim chance of ever walking again. 'But he's a tough son of a bitch, so it's no big surprise when he manages to beat that disability in the end,' said one fan of the show.

And there is an even more chilling side to police corruption in Arnott's old manor – guns. The character's south-east London upbringing would have likely made him extremely familiar with firearms. On those same mean streets, sawn-off shotguns and pistols have been commonplace for decades – long before the capital's current knife epidemic. So Arnott's childhood would have led to him coming across guns from a very young age. Many kids had fathers and uncles who used 'shooters' to hold up banks and security vans in the 1970s and 80s.

This may well have influenced Arnott's decision to train as a marksman with the police. During the *Line of Duty*'s five series to date, he even alludes to his happiest days being when he worked with the police's tactical fire arms unit, until he accidentally shot that man dead during a raid at the start of series one.

But if Arnott wears his heart on his sleeve thanks to his tough upbringing in a hotbed of crime, his AC-12 partner Kate Fleming could not be more different.

KATE FLEMING

Many viewers of *Line of Duty* have hailed AC-12 officer Kate Fleming (played by Vicky McClure) as being a prime example of a modern female officer in what remains quite an old-fashioned work environment. But it's really not as simple as that.

Kate Fleming is undoubtedly a much harder nut to crack than Steve Arnott. She doesn't speak her mind as much, for starters. She's a complex multi-layered character, who rarely gives away her true feelings about certain subjects.

According to Fleming's carefully constructed backstory, she was brought up by a single mother and they formed a close bond throughout her childhood. But that lonely childhood probably drove Kate to seek out a soulmate and husband too early in her development as an adult.

Kate's marriage problems are openly dealt with from the start of series one. Eventually she splits with her husband Mark, who is the father of her child. He even gets custody. No doubt this would have endeared her to AC-12 commanding officer Ted Hastings. He was looking for a strong independent female investigator with time to devote herself entirely to

The Job. Hastings would have considered these types of personal problems an advantage when it comes to working for AC-12.

Fleming's very special skill sets include an ability to go seamlessly undercover in order to shadow a corrupt police target. However, some ardent fans of *Line of Duty* believe she has her own reckless death wish because her duties so often find her entirely alone out on the front line of the fight against police corruption.

The makers of *Line of Duty* have even ensured that Fleming rapidly climbs the promotion ladder while Arnott fails over and over again to be promoted beyond sergeant. Yet many inside the real UK police feel this elevation of a relatively young female officer is unrealistic. One former detective explained: 'I guess the makers wanted women to do well, as they rightly should. But out here in the real police, men are still being promoted over women nine times out of ten.'

All this makes Kate Fleming an even more fascinating character. She's much more sly than even *in-yer-face* Arnott. She rarely mentions her own complicated home life. One fan said: 'Kate is a bit of a dark horse as a character and you want to know more about her choices outside The Job, but you also know she doesn't want to share much of that with anyone.'

Many real-world UK police detectives – who watch *Line of Duty* avidly – describe Kate as a 'well-rounded character'. One explained: 'Sure, she lets her husband have custody of their son but that's what so often happens with officers working inside sensitive units such as AC-12. It takes over your life, no two ways about it.'

Viewers of *Line of Duty* know full well that Arnott and Fleming have an ongoing and close friendship. In series one it resulted in a brief affair. Many are hoping that they get back together one day. One fan recently thought: 'I think the writers deliberately had Kate have subsequent romances and even later go back to her husband because they wanted to keep the audience guessing about her relationship with Steve.'

In the real world of policing, officers do have affairs with each other. But most are kept secret because they can make life inside a police unit extremely complicated, especially when targeting such a sensitive subject as police corruption. One recently retired south London detective explained: 'Being together in a police unit like AC-12 is extremely intense, so it's no surprise that Kate and Steve had that fling with each other. But Kate definitely handled it better than Steve. He is clearly smitten with Kate but she's the one who knows it's better not to continue the affair.

'Kate conducts herself admirably by even telling her bosses when she has an affair with another police officer in series two. It takes great courage to tell your boss about something like that, knowing it will mean you could be pulled out of an investigation early.'

It often seems as if Kate Fleming's number-one objective is keeping boss Ted Hastings happy. But then again, would he have really cared about her and Arnott having an affair in the first place?

And all this is part of what makes their boss the most complex *Line of Duty* character of all.

TED HASTINGS

The majority of real police officers who watch *Line of Duty* have a definitive favourite when it comes to the main characters – Ted Hastings. He's a multi-layered, unpredictable man who veers from one personal disaster to another, yet manages to hold his anti-corruption team together.

One moment he's inspiring them to bring down the bad cops in their midst. The next he's being seduced by a duplicitous, manipulative woman because his character can also be vulnerable and he also happens to be a sweetly old-fashioned gentleman.

Hastings' backstory is that he was born into desperate poverty in Northern Ireland and may even have been abused at the hands of some brutal adult or other. His father left his mother when he was a young child. No doubt Hastings learned the power of fear via a fist at a tender age just like his school friends, many of whom would end up on the wrong side of the law or, worse still, members of terror organisations. The young Ted Hastings had harboured an ambition to join the police since the age of twelve.

No wonder Hastings seems at first like an archetypal old-school copper. For all that, a more modern, sensitive side to his character soon emerges, which enables him to show genuine empathy to his friends, colleagues and even enemies.

Ted Hastings began his police career with the Royal Ulster Constabulary on the mean streets of Londonderry in Northern Ireland during the height of the so-called Troubles in the 1980s. That's when he witnessed first-hand the sort of blatant police corruption which helped convince him that one day he'd like to bring bad cops to justice. The RUC police force back then were frequently targeted by terrorists. Hastings was devastated when one of his best friends was killed in a pipe-bomb attack. There was also the constant threat of snipers and even remote-control bombs blowing up in the so-called bandit country of the border territories.

Real-life versions of Hastings would no doubt have been profoundly affected by the fatalities suffered in Northern Ireland. Many survivors of the conflict say the memories stay with them for their entire lives.

Ted Hastings and many of his law-abiding Northern Ireland police colleagues knew that there were corrupt officers amongst them who would most likely inform terrorists from the IRA and UDA where to find their best 'targets'. However, Hastings himself was a self-proclaimed 'straight shooter' appalled by the 'grey' aspects of Northern Ireland politics and policing.

The young Ted Hastings was by all accounts a lean and wiry character carefully trained to keep a low centre of gravity while moving through Northern Ireland's deadly streets, where danger seemed to lurk on every corner.

One former Northern Ireland police officer told me: 'You never switched off back then. You watched everyone's back all the time. Being on the streets of Northern Ireland taught you not to trust anyone. The IRA wanted to kill as many police officers as they could. It sometimes really was a matter of kill or be killed.'

RUC officers like Hastings were trained specifically in

how to deal with interrogation by the 'enemy' should they be captured or kidnapped. Officers were taught to believe they'd never crack in the face of any violent threats, however harsh. Those skills would come in very handy when Hastings found himself interrogating allegedly corrupt cops as chief of *Line of Duty*'s AC-12 anti-corruption unit.

Police officers in Northern Ireland were constantly being accused of using excessive force and deliberately destroying religious objects in homes they searched. There's no doubt that some of Hastings' colleagues would have been guilty of this and other – even more questionable acts – during the Troubles. But Hastings prided himself on never stooping that low. A mistake made by a young RUC officer on the streets of Londonderry or Belfast could plunge Northern Ireland into chaos or bring down the government in London. It really was as serious as that.

But there was another consequence of Hastings' experiences in Northern Ireland. His senses would have been deadened in many ways by the cold-blooded nature of the violence, as many police officers and soldiers who've served in conflict zones would attest. One explained: 'When bullets are flying all around you and you know the locals would love nothing more than to kill you, it certainly makes you more careful when it comes to trusting people. You learn to sometimes not look on people as human beings but as constant threats to your existence.' Nevertheless, Ted Hastings would never have become embroiled in the RUC's classic corruption practices, which often involved brutal treatment of suspects and a twisted form of dealing with crime.

Hastings – like all young RUC officers at that time – would have heard rumours about how renegade officers had secretly joined Protestant death squads. How other fellow RUC officers were so closely linked to The Cause that they'd happily tip off IRA units about police activities, putting their own colleagues at great risk.

Ultimately, Ted Hastings is the fatherly figure who steers AC-12 in the right direction. Or at least he tries to.

Hastings' experiences in Northern Ireland would also have fuelled his constant use of gallows humour to cope with some very dangerous moments. This helps endear him greatly to his *Line of Duty* audience as well as his AC-12 colleagues. Even when he admonishes his team for some grave mistake or other, he can't help doing it with a kindly, parental smile on his face, most of the time.

THE THIN BLUE LINE

As commanding officer of AC-12, Ted Hastings treads a thin blue line between being father figure to his detectives, including Fleming and Arnott, and giving them 'severe bollockings' when they step out of line. But it must all seem pretty tame compared to what he was used to when he was a young rookie officer in Northern Ireland.

Many real-life police officers believe that Hastings' disturbing experiences in Northern Ireland might well have prevented him from moving 'across the water' to serve with the UK mainland police in the 1990s. 'The Troubles are one hell of a big piece of baggage for a copper to carry around,' said one retired detective. 'I'm not sure he'd have been considered steady enough to even be encouraged to join any of the mainland police forces, let alone an anti-corruption unit.'

Other police officers completely disagree. They insist Hastings' background would have made him even better prepared to deal with the enormous pressures of working inside such a controversial department. 'Ted Hastings is a classic Marmite character. You either love him or hate him,' explained one former officer. 'In one sense, he's a severely screwed-up guy, but he's used all those experiences to help him and his team. I wish my own superior officers had been as multi-layered as Hastings when I was a copper because your background should not stain your ability to be a good cop.'

However, Ted Hastings' frankness and honesty does sometimes make him vulnerable to duplicitous characters such as AC-12's Detective Inspector 'Dot' Cotton, who uses his membership of the unit for his own corrupt activities. 'Hastings took a long time to suss out Dot Cotton,' said one former detective. 'Sometimes, he can be incredibly naïve because he doesn't like pre-judging people like most cops do. I suppose that's why he recruits "different and interesting" characters like Fleming and Arnott.'

Hastings stubbornly refuses to condemn the secretly evil Dot Cotton, despite being urged to do so by his team. 'At one stage, Hastings was like putty in the hands of Dot Cotton,' added the same former detective. 'Hastings wanted to believe that no officer of his could be corrupt. He saw it as a slight on his abilities as a senior officer.'

The same former detective added: 'I worked for someone

just like Hastings, who thought the best of everyone. I watched so many of my colleagues manipulate him. Sometimes it was extremely frustrating for me because I could see he was being taken for a ride, but he refused to accept it.'

At one stage during *Line of Duty* series five, it seems likely that Hastings is in fact the evil 'H', a corrupt officer on the unit who's causing death and destruction throughout all of the series.

He wasn't H but that storyline helped highlight a problem that many officers working in anti-corruption units experience. Basically they couldn't trust anyone, not even their most trusted colleagues and boss.

As a result, anti-corruption officers are often left with no option but to go undercover in order to nail down suspected bent cops.

WHAT LIES BENEATH

Line of Duty's Steve Arnott and Kate Fleming frequently work undercover and it is often fraught with danger.

One former south London detective explained: 'When you go undercover that's it. You're on your own a lot of the time. You have to immerse yourself in the character you're pretending to be.' And in real life you often have to be an even better actor than those star performers in *Line of Duty* because one slip-up could cost you your life.

Indeed, undercover police operations are sometimes so secretive that commanding officers are professionally obliged to virtually abandon their undercover officers, so as not to risk them being identified. One retired detective recalled: 'That can be very tough if you're out in the field alone. It leads to a feeling of complete isolation. No one can even acknowledge what you're doing.'

And in the real-life police, in the same way Stephen Graham's undercover character John Corbett blurs the lines of his undercover mission, some officers have even ended up becoming corrupt *after* going undercover. One former detective explained: 'I know of some officers who went undercover on dangerous investigations and turned corrupt themselves. Initially they'd done it in order to convince criminals they were genuine. But on each occasion, they actually ended up properly going over to the other side.'

The same former detective then talked through one case which sounded as if it had come straight out of a *Line of Duty* storyline. The detective recalled: 'We had a young female officer who'd volunteered to go undercover inside a club run by the Turkish mafia in north London.' The female officer, he said, was told not to compromise herself but she ended up sleeping with a number of gangsters in order to remain 'authentic' to her mission.

'Amazingly, her senior officers actually thought this was okay and defended it by saying it was an essential part of remaining undercover. After all, they said, these gangsters were extremely dangerous,' he continued. 'But no one told her she had to have sex with men when she volunteered to go undercover. In my opinion, she should have been pulled out of that operation immediately this was known.'

'Her superior officers should be ashamed of themselves

because they turned a blind eye to it all. All they cared about was making sure they collected enough evidence to arrest the main criminals.'

But then it got worse. 'This undercover officer told us that two other gangsters had raped her,' added the detective. When she told her police bosses they pointed out that if they arrested the criminals in question, it would blow her cover and they might well try and kill her. 'So this poor female officer had no option but to stay undercover, even after that appalling ordeal. She was in a very distressed state by this stage and it undoubtedly weakened her own resolve.'

But the female officer's bosses were convinced she could cope and left her out in the field, despite everything that had happened. Then – unknown to this undercover officer's bosses – she became close to another gangster. The same detective recalled: 'He was so appalled when she told him about the rape that he had the two rapists beaten up and almost killed, although none of us knew this was happening at the time.'

The same female undercover officer eventually let slip to her bosses that she'd slept with the gangster. The detective recalled: 'Her senior officers finally tried to get her out of the operation but she insisted she was fine and could carry on.'

Unknown to the police, the woman undercover officer had already told her new gangster lover that she was a police officer. 'She obviously felt more affinity for him than her colleagues because he sympathised so much about her rape. I think he may even have been genuinely in love with her.'

The gangster even assured the woman officer he didn't care about her being an undercover police officer. The detective went on: 'But then he got her to agree to be his eyes and ears inside the police. I suppose you could say she was obliged to become a corrupt cop. But a lot of us felt very sorry for her.'

So this same woman officer continued submitting reports to her police bosses, while supposedly working undercover. Only a strange twist of fate led to her eventually being exposed.

The same detective went on: 'One of the men who raped her in the first place became a police informant. He revealed the full story because he was so upset with the way his boss had treated him.'

But before this undercover woman officer could be removed from the operation, she disappeared. 'At first it was feared she'd been killed by the gang. But then we received credible information that she'd gone to Turkey with her lover, got herself a new identity, married him and they were living in a seaside resort in the south of the country.'

The same detective added: 'Myself and many of my colleagues felt extremely sorry for this woman officer. She'd been left completely exposed and all alone without any proper support. In some ways I don't blame her for going rogue in the end. Where else could she turn? How can you remain loyal if your own bosses are so prepared to ignore your safety?'

Sometimes, officers investigating police corruption face huge sacrifices and the ultimate smears.

TRUMPED-UP CHARGES

In series three of *Line of Duty*, Detective Constable Steve Arnott is accused of being the gangland informant and corrupt cop known as 'The Caddy'. It's one of a series of ongoing storylines which have gripped the programme's vast audience throughout every series of the show. Arnott also finds himself framed for the murder of psychotic corrupt cop Lindsay Denton.

In real life, anti-corruption officers often face trumped-up charges because they're considered 'rats' by many regular, even law-abiding, fellow officers. Anti-corruption officers themselves know only too well that such allegations unfortunately 'come with the territory'.

One recently retired anti-corruption detective expanded on this: 'You're hated by both sides if you work in an anti-corruption unit. In other words, you're damned if you do and you're damned if you don't. It's as simple as that. You should be trained to cope with false accusations before you even start work in anti-corruption. But it's often not the criminals that one has to fear but the bent coppers who will do anything to stop you if they think you're about to expose them.'

Police officers of all ranks look on smears by criminals as being part of the job. But when so-called 'straight officers' threaten anti-corruption investigators for investigating bent cops, it's even harder to handle. Another recently retired detective explained to me: 'There is an attitude of no smoke without fire. But that is so misleading because many accusations of corruption turn out to be completely without foundation. However, the investigative system inside the police means that no stone can be left unturned, even if you're clearly 99 per cent innocent of any accusation.'

One of my sources told me that, in the summer of 2019, an

unnamed anti-corruption officer on one UK police force was accused of sexually abusing his own niece. It later emerged she'd been pressurised by criminals to make the complaint.

One of the detectives involved in the investigation later explained: 'There was absolutely no evidence to back up this girl's claims. We even knew that one of the officer's relatives was a criminal and the two had fallen out because they were on opposing sides of the law. It was an appalling situation. This officer was married with three children and he was being accused of sexually abusing a thirteen-year-old schoolgirl.

'Even worse still, other officers with scores to settle then jumped on the bandwagon because this particular detective was not the most popular guy in the world, especially since he had at one stage worked for an anti-corruption unit.

'Most of us knew it had to be a put-up job. But that poor bastard had to be psychologically assessed. He even took a polygraph, which he passed. And a lot of sensitive stuff about his childhood and private life came to light during the investigation. But nothing he'd done broke the law. In fairness to him, he was 100 per cent co-operative with investigators and never tried to hide anything about his private life.'

The officer even admitted to a therapist that he himself had been sexually abused when he was a child. But then some senior officers jumped on this as being proof that he was capable of abusing a child himself because of the trauma he'd suffered.

The same detective added: 'To call it a witch hunt is an understatement. That guy was being hung, drawn and quartered and he clearly hadn't done anything wrong.'

The case was eventually dropped because the so-called victim withdrew her statement to police after her father was recorded referring to the accusations as false. This same officer's relative later admitted he'd convinced his own daughter she'd been abused by the officer. 'That man should have been prosecuted for, at the very least, wasting police time,' the same detective believed. 'But the officer in question begged his superiors to drop everything for the sake of his family.'

That officer never recovered. He was transferred off the anti-corruption unit and given a desk job. The same detective added: 'He split up with his wife and his kids can't get what he was accused of out of their heads. Poor bastard.'

RELATIONSHIPS

Millions of *Line of Duty* viewers have seen Kate Fleming's marriage crumbling in heartbreaking circumstances. Ted Hastings ends up living in a hotel room after splitting up with his wife, and Steve Arnott veers from relationship to relationship after an acrimonious break-up with his long-term police detective girlfriend. It's part of the reason why we feel so connected to the characters as viewers.

Many real-life police officers have pointed out that problems at home can often have a profound effect on an officer's abilities as an investigator. One serving police detective told me: 'If your home life is falling apart then it's doubly hard to be an effective copper.'

Steve Arnott perfectly reflects this problem because he's

desperate to settle down and get some security in his home life but he just can't manage it. As a result, he seems destined to be one of those eternal bachelor types, constantly trying to find domestic bliss without realising that it's almost too late now he's in his mid-thirties.

Many real-life officers also insist that being 'settled down' could even help prevent many instances of police corruption in the long term. One explained: 'I had this great mate who was a bit of a Jack the Lad. He just wouldn't or couldn't settle down.

'But all his drinking and womanising – he was even taking cocaine – caught up with him in the end. He owed some dealer money and found himself in a corner, so he accepted a bribe. That was the beginning of the end for him. But it would never have happened if his life hadn't been so chaotic.'

Clearly, there are many reasons why police officers go crooked, but having an extra-marital affair with a colleague is probably the most damaging, especially if both are anti-corruption officers.

IN-HOUSE AFFAIRS

In the real world of policing, officers admit that affairs in the workplace are nearly always kept secret because they are 'deal-breakers' when it comes to being a police officer.

'And that's a problem in itself,' explained one detective. 'Because as a copper you're supposed to be upfront about everything that's going on in your life.'

No doubt 'in-house' relationships can also make detectives

on a police corruption unit like AC-12 extremely vulnerable to pressure from outside influences.

As another detective explained: 'I remember one colleague of mine fell for another officer, even though they were both married. At first, we all laughed about it because they were like a couple of lovelorn teenagers. But gradually they started to get more secretive about it, especially after pretending the relationship had ended.

'It was typical extramarital stuff, I guess. But then we discovered that both of them were being blackmailed by a criminal who'd found out about their affair and was threatening to tell their partners.'

The female officer immediately ended the affair but the criminal still threatened to make sure her husband found out, unless she agreed to accept bribes in exchange for 'favours'.

The same detective continued: 'Then she restarted the affair with the other officer. But the husband of this woman officer then found out by accident that his wife was having the affair.'

The husband confronted his wife and then informed the wife of her lover. The husband was so upset, he tried to take his own life because he thought his wife was going to run away with her lover.

'But nothing could be further from the truth. In the end, the officers broke up permanently and stayed married to their respective partners. The criminal was eventually trapped by this couple's anti-police corruption unit colleagues, who recorded him making threatening phone calls to both officers.'

Senior officers decided not to prosecute the two lovers for leaking information to the criminal because of the 'extreme circumstances' of the case.

No doubt such issues will continue to be debated for as long as *Line of Duty* is screened. And many real-life junior officers accuse senior officers of sending out mixed messages when it comes to such incidents.

But what's it actually like being married to a corrupt police officer?

THE OTHER HALF

Being the live-in partner of a police officer is never easy, but when they're leading a double life because of real-life corruption similar to storylines that have gripped millions of TV viewers on *Line of Duty*, then it must be doubly hard.

One wife of a senior Flying Squad detective who worked during The Sweeney's wild days from the 1970s through to the 1990s once told me: 'It's tough enough being married to a cop who puts The Job first, but when they're also secretly corrupt, it's hell.

'Back in the day, there was no therapy or advice to get from anyone if you had marriage problems.

'My husband was regularly working eighteen-, even sometimes twenty-hour days, and then he'd come home half-cut after unwinding on a skinful in the pub. I often smelt perfume on him and he'd claim he'd had to handcuff some woman and that's why he stank. But I knew he was lying to me a lot of the time.

'But what I didn't realise was that he was trying to cope with the added pressure of being corrupt as well.'

It was an era, as we've already seen, when police officers often got their best results by treading a thin line between the underworld and the police world. One of that same detective's best informants at the time was a madam who ran a notorious brothel in the West End of London. Her clients ranged from criminals to politicians and she was paying the detective bribes via her crime boss.

The officer's wife explained: 'After a while I started to wonder if my husband was falling in love with this woman because he used to talk about her a lot. Then gradually he told me less and less about her and that made me even more suspicious.'

Every time this officer came home late, claiming he'd been on a surveillance operation, his wife sensed he was lying. But she didn't have the courage to challenge him because 'he seemed to have the problems of the world on his shoulders.'

However, this police marriage-from-hell came to a head when the brothel madam turned up unexpectedly at the detective's family home.

His wife takes up the story: 'The moment I opened the door, I knew it was her. She asked if my husband was in. I tried to act cool and said he was at work.'

Then the woman calmly pulled something out of her pocket. The wife at first thought it was a gun. Then she realised it was more like a pen. In fact, it was a pregnancy-testing device. The woman threw it on the doorstep in front of the officer's wife and stormed off.

'I packed a suitcase with a few of my husband's clothes, had the locks changed and left the case on our doorstep for him to take when he got home.'

The couple never went to counselling. The wife simply filed for divorce. And that marked the beginning of the end of that once highly regarded police detective.

His now ex-wife explained: 'He fell apart. He turned even more to drink and his career crumbled. He ended up being busted for taking bribes, took early retirement on a half pension and worked as a taxi driver.

'The worst thing about it all is that if it had been now then maybe, just maybe, we might have salvaged the marriage because I still love him to this day, despite everything. He had a lot of issues like any copper but maybe we could have worked through them.'

The officer never went near his mistress again and she had an abortion.

'So we ended up with two shattered lives and two heartbroken children, who just wanted their parents to live happily ever after,' his ex-wife concluded.

No doubt corruption played a huge role in that crumbling marriage.

CATCH-22

In *Line of Duty*, police corruption follows very much a linear path, giving viewers the clear impression that corrupt officers think they can play the system. In real life, it is much the same.

Many crooked cops have come unstuck because they believed they could manipulate criminals by 'rewarding' them for information and then getting those same criminals to pay them bribes in return.

One recently retired detective explained: 'A lot of coppers fall into this trap. They underestimate how manipulative criminals can be. I know a number of good detectives who thought they could get the most information out of their criminal sources by doing something corrupt to "reward" them for their help.'

One classic example occurred when a big-time drug baron began feeding information to a detective he knew. This officer never once questioned the criminal's motivation. 'Yet this gangster was stitching up his enemies, so he could take an even bigger slice of the drug market,' the same detective added.

The compromised officer even agreed to search the police's national computer for details on one of that criminal's enemies. 'He didn't even think about the consequences of those actions. Of course, this compromised that officer immediately and he became like putty in the hands of this villain.'

But when the same corrupt officer ended up being exposed as a bent cop, he claimed he'd been nurturing that criminal and had actually done nothing wrong.

The detective explained: 'I actually believed him and so did many of my colleagues. But he'd been incredibly naïve because that sort of action nearly always ends in disaster, if you're not careful.'

HATTON GARDEN

Line of Duty revolves around fictional storylines that often take their inspiration from the real underworld. But sometimes the most headline-hitting crimes can flag up unexpected crooked cop connections.

There's even a link between corrupt police and the legendary Hatton Garden gang of robbers, who pulled off the UK's so-called 'crime of the century' in April 2015. The gang stole in the region of £14 million worth of cash and valuables from an underground safe deposit facility in London's Hatton Garden.

The heist was planned and carried out by six elderly professional criminals, all of whom pleaded guilty and received prison sentences in March 2016. Four other men were also tried on suspicion of involvement: three were found guilty and sent to prison, while the fourth was cleared.

But back in 1993, one of the criminals who was jailed for the Hatton Garden Job stood trial with two allegedly corrupt police officers. They'd teamed up with another gangster in a bid to recover £600,000 owed to the same man by an underworld financier, not realising the entire transaction had been secretly filmed.

The gang were eventually caught by police corruption busters from a real-life version of *Line of Duty*'s AC-12 unit. One criminal was seen bragging how he'd beat the debtor with an iron bar while trying to make him pay him the £80,000. That same criminal ended up being jailed for four years for his role in the plot. The two corrupt officers were also jailed.

Police corruption can come in all shapes and sizes.

LADDERING

In *Line of Duty* series one, crooked cop Tony Gates (played by Lennie James) is suspected of 'laddering' – a technique in which different charges are placed on the same defendant in order to increase the number of a particular officer's successful convictions. It's the law enforcement equivalent of cricket ball-tampering.

In the real world, this practice has only recently been clamped down on because computer records make it much harder for bent officers to fake their paperwork.

The series-one storyline involving Gates' laddering offences was eventually overshadowed by the murderous activities of local professional criminal Tommy Hunter. His money-laundering operation sparked a gang war which saw Gates become the target for blackmailers until he agreed to help AC-12 to try and bring Hunter to justice.

As Gates' professional and private life crumbles, he leaves a trail of evidence for his anti-corruption pursuers. It's almost as if he wants to be brought to justice in order to end his ordeal.

Not surprisingly, in the actual police world, this type of pressure can often build up until there is an implosion.

BROKE AND VULNERABLE

In series two of *Line of Duty*, woman officer Lindsay Denton (played by Keeley Hawes) is one of the show's most talked-about characters. Denton is seriously in debt, looking after an elderly mother and sees no alternative but to go on the take.

It's a familiar excuse made by many real-life corrupt police officers. One former detective explained: 'More needs to be done to monitor police officers' finances because going broke is the biggest single motivating factor when it comes to corrupt cops.'

Today, police officers are being encouraged to tell their superiors if they have money problems to prevent them getting out of control. But as one former detective pointed out: 'That's all very well, but who wants to admit they're broke, especially to their own bosses? Coppers are no different from anyone else in that regard. I don't know what the answer is, but there needs to be an efficient yet sensitive system in place, which enables officers with financial problems to come forward and talk about it without feeling shame.'

COMPLIANCE

Many viewers of *Line of Duty* have been surprised that this gritty urban drama is located in an un-named city. The first series was actually filmed on location in Birmingham but it was then moved to Belfast.

I'm told this is partly because Northern Ireland has a very generous filming subsidy system (ask the *Game of Thrones* producers). Also, Belfast and other cities have a wide range of locations which enable *Line of Duty* to continue to be set in an anonymous urban setting.

But there is another reason behind the decision not to specify what force the corruption busters from AC-12 belong to. The programme makers have an obligation to 'water down' any awkward coincidences that might lead real-life officers to presume a specific police force or individual is being identified.

As one insider from the series told me: 'If they'd located the series in, say, London or Manchester, then it would have also narrowed down the appeal to potential audiences. But even more importantly, there are legal compliance issues to consider as well.

'Having the series located in a fictional city ensures that no one can accuse the writers of basing any of the characters on a living person, which could then could provoke legal action that might prove immensely costly.'

To put this in laymen's terms, *Line of Duty*'s storylines are so close to real life that the BBC insists on making sure there are no legal comebacks from any 'real-life overlaps' that might have inspired the storylines in the show.

As one *Line of Duty* insider explained: 'It's ironic because the show thrives on its "authentic feel", which has been one of the key elements of its success. The audience needs to believe in the characters and the plotlines, so it's inevitable that some real police officers might feel their stories are being told in *Line of Duty*, even when this is not the case.'

So far, *Line of Duty* has not been sued by any living police officers or anyone else claiming that characters in the programme are based on them. However, the show's team of legal advisors continues to work around the clock, reading scripts and checking footage before, during and after production of the programme to ensure this will never happen.

'If someone sued the programme, the entire production could end up being shut down,' one member of the *Line of Duty* crew clarified. 'That would also mean re-filming scenes and changing plotlines, which could cost the BBC millions of pounds.'

The fact this hasn't happened is a credit to the professionalism of the programme's writers, producers and directors.

No wonder many inside the TV industry believe *Line of Duty* may end up being the longest-running police series in UK television history.

ART IMITATES LIFE

Line of Duty prides itself on its simple storylines, which have no doubt helped the show become the most popular cop drama in UK television history.

It's been reported that series creator Jed Mercurio is a keen fan of one of the first ever police procedural TV drama series, *Hill Street Blues*, first aired in the 1970s.

One of the most popular episodes of all time was called 'Freedom's Last Stand' and centred around police corruption. Always ahead of its time, HSB managed to handle the sensitive issue of crooked cops in a way never before seen on the small screen.

Another inspiration for *Line of Duty* would no doubt have been LA-based cop drama *The Shield*, which premiered in 2002. Somehow lead detective Vic Mackey manages to illicit sympathy from the audience, even though he is overtly corrupt on most levels and would most definitely have found himself investigated by AC-12 for crooked activities that even included murder.

On top of this, Mackey also has an affair with a heroin-addicted hooker, pays off other police officers and covers up another murder. Yet he still manages to be a loveable character. As one serving detective later explained: '*The Shield* was seen as wildly over the top by most real cops. But that's because Mackey was such a brilliant character that he made you face up to your own demons.'

Another TV cop drama which has undoubtedly influenced *Line of Duty* is the ground-breaking US TV series *The Wire*, which helped launch the acting career of British actor Idris Elba, as well as many others, when it was first screened back in 2002.

The Wire was created and primarily written by author and former police reporter David Simon. Set and produced in Baltimore, Maryland, *The Wire* introduced a different institution of the city and its relationship to law enforcement in each season, while retaining characters and advancing storylines from previous seasons. It's a storytelling method used to great effect in *Line of Duty*.

The Wire was lauded for its literary themes, its uncommonly accurate exploration of society and politics, and its realistic portrayal of urban life. Although during its original run the series received only average ratings and never won any major television awards, it is now widely regarded as one of the greatest TV shows of all time.

SUSPENDING DISBELIEF

Line of Duty creator Jed Mercurio has frequently stated that many of his storylines for *Line of Duty* are inspired by a wide range of real-life UK crimes.

In series three of *Line of Duty*, the show enters into this territory when the storyline revolves around a paedophile ring linked to Jimmy Savile. The onetime TV presenter's exposé as a rampant paedophile only came to light after his death in 2011, so using his name in connection with a gang of sexual predators was a brave decision.

Another true-crime case that influenced the show was that of Stefan Kiszko, a twenty-three-year-old loner imprisoned for a murder he never committed after corrupt officers framed him. He was cleared of the murder and released from prison eighteen years later. Jed Mercurio has admitted he was fascinated by the case and the corruption issues connected to it.

The writers of *Line of Duty* have cleverly thrown all sorts of dramatic devices into the show and they usually work well because of the viewer's ability to suspend disbelief. In other words, fans get so immersed in the drama that even the most outrageous scenes feel believable to a mainstream audience.

But, obviously, real-life police officers do not always swallow these sorts of storylines because they've lived much more than what is being portrayed on the small screen. As a consequence of this, some highly critical police officers say that *Line of Duty* is not an accurate reflection of today's UK police forces.

Senior officers working inside anti-corruption units similar to the show's fictional AC-12 say that the methods used to vet officers and staff, investigate complaints and misconduct are inaccurate and unbelievable. Some have even condemned the series for 'bearing no resemblance to reality'.

Real-life police officers have cited as a classic example how *Line of Duty* officers being investigated for corruption do not have the right to be interviewed by someone at least one rank above them. This happens frequently on the TV show, yet serving officers say it's 'highly unlikely' a superintendent would be the one doing the interviews.

They've also criticised the way that officers on *Line of Duty* seem able to literally grab hold of a firearm in the office without any safety system being in place. 'You can't just grab a weapon and fly out the door,' one retired Flying Squad officer explained. 'You have to get written permission, go to the weapons store and then sign for it. Then go somewhere else for the ammunition. It's a proper process.'

Another alleged inaccuracy in the show is the way that senior officers wear dress uniforms while interviewing suspects. One serving officer explained: 'That simply does not happen. I know it makes no difference to the essence of the story as far as the audience is concerned, but it matters to real coppers.'

As a result of these alleged inaccuracies, some police organisations in the UK, including the Independent Police Complaints Commission (now called the Independent Office for Police Conduct) and Scotland Yard, have refused to co-operate with the makers of *Line of Duty*.

Other serving officers say there are further examples where *Line of Duty* has stretched plausibility.

In *Line of Duty* series four, we meet woman detective Roz Huntley (played by Thandie Newton). She deliberately opens a complex police crime-busting operation at the same time as being investigated by corruption busters AC-12. But in the real world of policing, it would be virtually impossible for two such operations to run parallel with each other. One officer explained: 'It just doesn't happen. I'm disappointed when I see these sort of inaccuracies because that means the public are not always getting a fair and balanced picture of police corruption through *Line of Duty*.'

Another overall aspect of the programme that irritates the police is the way that AC-12 officers appear to be able to make up their own rules as they go along. This can lead to them breaking into people's homes and even threatening members of the public. None of this would happen in real life, insist some officers.

One senior serving police officer said: 'It's vital that people out there realise that real police officers have to abide by a strict code of conduct and ethics. This means not committing criminal offences as we often see happening in *Line of Duty*.'

As is so often the case, real police officers also insist that corruption is nowhere near as commonplace as it's portrayed in *Line of Duty*. The show's police advisors even admit that serving officers do regularly complain about the content of the TV series.

But *Line of Duty* executives insist the series does not show policing in a wholly negative light, despite the accusations.

One of them explained: 'Everyone is entitled to their own opinion of the programme, especially the police. But *Line of Duty* is a drama series, not a documentary. And the great advantage of drama is that it doesn't always have to be 100 per cent accurate, especially if that slows down the drama. After all, this is what keeps the viewers glued to their TV sets.'

Another senior BBC executive recently told me: 'We appreciate why some police officers are frustrated by *Line of Duty*. But our main priority is to entertain the audience. Moving the action forward at great pace sometimes leads to scenes which are there for that specific purpose. They're not always 100 per cent accurate about real-life policing. I'm afraid there is nothing we can do about that.'

But is repressing the *real* facts about police corruption in the UK just as disturbing?

Chapter Three

ON THE STREETS

'I've said it before and I'll say it again. Catching criminals is tough enough but catching coppers – God give me strength.'

Ted Hastings in *Line of Duty*

THE 'COVER-UP'

The real police continue to be as reluctant as ever to talk openly about the true extent of corruption inside UK police forces, even in these supposedly more open times. UK police forces insist there have never been more than 65 allegations of misconduct per 1,000 officers at any one time and the vast majority of those offences are described as having been 'minor misdemeanours'.

Yet recent figures show that more than 300 police officers and police community support officers in the UK have been convicted of offences over the past three years. And despite those claims to the contrary by the police, these offences are serious and include sex crimes, assaults and possessing indecent images of children.

But here's the double whammy: only 25 of the UK's 45 police forces actually provided figures following a recent Freedom of Information request by journalists. The 20 forces that did not provide information either said they could not reveal the number of convictions because of the cost of retrieving the information, or simply did not even bother to respond to the request. Police Scotland and the Police Service of Northern Ireland were amongst those who failed to provide the required information.

As one renowned crime correspondent said: 'The police need to get real about this. You'd think *Line of Duty* might make them sit up and take notice. They can't keep pulling the wool over all our eyes. It doesn't wash in this day and age.

'It feels as if the old, familiar police denial reactions to corruption are still lingering in the air. The police need to be 100 per cent transparent about all these corruption issues before it's too late. The police are clearly damaging themselves by being so unwilling to be open about corruption.'

Further figures obtained in 2019 under that same Freedom of Information request showed there had been 189 convictions of corrupt officers across the UK. Northern Ireland had the worst record, with 57 offences committed by serving officers, including possession of a loaded firearm while drunk, supplying Class B and C drugs and selling counterfeit goods.

Greater Manchester Police was the second most corrupt force, with 32 convictions for crimes, including voyeurism and outraging public decency, sexual activity with a child under 16, possessing indecent images of a child, supplying Class A drugs and even murder.

As one recently retired officer explained: 'Until all the UK police forces come out and provide figures, the public will believe that we're happier hiding the reality of police corruption than dealing with it. No wonder shows like *Line of Duty* are so popular. We should be using its success to encourage more openness but instead many forces are battening down the hatches and trying to push the entire subject off the public agenda.'

No wonder there is even further evidence that some UK police forces will continue to ignore the facts regarding corruption.

BURIED IN THE SAND

Inside Scotland Yard's DPS – today's real-life version of AC-12 – officers from the Anti-Corruption Command (ACC) are supposed to investigate allegations and intelligence relating to corrupt police officers and staff or those that seek to corrupt their staff.

Yet many officers suspected of links to crime syndicates have in the past kept their jobs inside the ACC and – in some cases – even continued being directly involved in investigations into organised crime.

Ten years ago, a source of mine told me that one detective was moved from the ACC to a police station in north-east London because of suspicions he might be linked to organised crime. That same officer – who served on the criminal informant 'source unit' of the ACC – was then moved to another police station in London, where he once again was given full clearance to access computer data across the capital. Yet this same officer was still suspected of working for a crime syndicate, as well as being part of a wider network of corrupt officers.

When this particular detective was eventually transferred once again, his superiors were told to 'find a use for him but don't allow him to access any intelligence systems'. However, this order was apparently ignored and within months, the same crooked officer was once again selling sensitive information to criminals after his access to intelligence was reinstated.

And there is one particular corner of England which has become a 'hotspot' for police corruption.

Welcome to…

THE GARDEN OF ENGLAND

Rolling fields of golden corn, converted oast houses, luscious green pastures… Kent is supposed to be the ideal of what the countryside should be: peaceful, winding country lanes, filled with modest folk minding their own business, motivated by a love of gardening, but certainly nothing as vulgar as money.

But lurking in amongst the unprepossessing villages of this quintessential English county have been some of the biggest names from the British underworld and their shadowy police associates.

Kent has a long history of crime going back to the highway robbers of the sixteenth and seventeenth centuries. But in the late 1970s and well into the 1980s, a number of 'minted' south London gangsters set up home in often isolated mansions between the south London suburbs and the channel ports of Dover and Folkestone.

The National Criminal Intelligence Service estimated that there was a hard core of about 200 'Premier League' criminals in Britain at that time. At least one third of them owned property in Kent and south-east London and most had corrupt cops on their payroll.

One such Kent criminal was 'Big Al' Decabral. He was a police informer at the highest level, one who also boasted of having some pretty high-powered cops in his pocket. He had associates inside the underworld and the police and he liked nothing more than to play them all off against each other.

Decabral was a supplier of illegal arms. However, he often also provided information to his favourite police friends, and in the early autumn of 2000, he told them some juicy details about one of the so-called masterminds behind the Brink's-Mat robbery.

That was to prove a big mistake.

On Thursday, 5 October 2000, Decabral was heaving his twenty-stone frame into the passenger seat of his son's Peugeot with great difficulty in the car park of a Halfords store, in Ashford, Kent. He was more used to driving around in his own vintage Jag, once owned by legendary gangster Reggie Kray.

But just as Decabral checked the time on his gold Rolex, a man holding a gun equipped with a silencer pulled alongside him in another car. Decabral briefly pleaded for his life but then two shots rang out and his vast, blubbery body slumped against the steering wheel of that tiny Peugeot, setting off the car's horn. Terrified shoppers fled.

Decabral had been targeted after corrupt detectives tipped off the same criminal mastermind he'd just grassed up. It's also believed that those same crooked officers even provided associates of that gangster boss with Decabral's movements, which so conveniently led to that hitman in the shopping centre car park.

A few miles from where Decabral was murdered was the village of West Kingsdown, probably representing the most classic example of the way criminals had laid their own territorial stake in the heart of Middle England. For almost thirty years, West Kingsdown was the home of one of the UK's most notorious criminals. This character was a real-life equivalent of mobster Tommy Hunter, the ghost-like crime boss behind much of the corruption featured in the first three series of *Line of Duty*.

With a population of 5,400, West Kingsdown – just twenty-five miles from London – had a disproportionately large number of mock Tudor mansions with long driveways, immaculate high brick walls, sophisticated closed-circuit TV, electronically operated gates and at least two Rottweilers on duty.

Following the lucrative Brink's-Mat robbery in 1983, undercover police carried out surveillance on a house on the outskirts of West Kingsdown. Officers observed one criminal involved with the heist taking bars of gold out of the boot of this car in the driveway of his detached home. This same gangster was even converting a barn on his property into a metal-smelting works. For weeks there had been rumours that corrupt detectives had informed this gangster he was being watched.

Another of West Kingsdown's criminal residents – who'd often talked openly about his own crooked police officers – lived in a detached house in the village. This same criminal's common-law wife had even herself served time inside prison for her role in the aftermath of the Brinks' Mat gold bullion raid.

When I tried to talk to this woman through her electronically operated gates, I was greeted by two Rottweilers (I didn't catch their names) and a few terse words spoken through the crackling intercom as she examined my face on a closed-circuit TV screen. Later, I was phoned by a serving detective who warned me to keep away from this woman and her associates. He made it sound like he was doing me a favour. I assumed he was more likely 'in the pocket' of these criminals.

Around the same time, wealthy Kent car dealer John Marshall, thirty-four, sold one of the Brink's-Mat gang some false number plates before he was found shot dead. He was slumped in his black Range Rover in Sydenham, Kent, near West Kingsdown. Marshall was known to be close to several police officers.

Then there was alleged criminal Keith Hedley. He was

killed by supposed bandits on his yacht in Corfu in September 1996. Hedley, fifty-seven, was a suspected money launderer with many police 'friends' who had a penchant for living the good life. Years later, I was told that corrupt detectives had supplied criminals with the location of Hedley's boat.

Then came Kent resident Nick Whiting. He was stabbed nine times and then shot twice with a 9 mm pistol in June 1990. Whiting, forty-three, owned a detached house in Ightham, Kent, and had bank accounts containing more than a million pounds when he died. There was clear evidence Whiting had met with a corrupt police officer a few days before his body was found on Rainham Marshes, in Essex.

One of the most legendary incidents in Kent's underworld history occurred when pub landlord George Francis was shot by a hooded gunman in May 1985, but survived. Francis was a well-known figure in the south-east London underworld who often entertained corrupt police officers at his pub.

But of course there are other parts of the UK where police corruption is also prevalent.

THE BIRMINGHAM CONNECTION

Line of Duty series one was filmed on locations in Birmingham in the UK's centre. In real life, this part of the country has been a hotbed of criminality going back to before the reign of the street gangs which inspired another hit TV show, *Peaky Blinders*.

In the late 1960s and early 1970s the spectre of police corruption existed in Birmingham on a vast scale. But this wasn't just so-called 'bobbies on the beat' being 'given a drink', as criminals called bribes back in those days.

One notorious young Birmingham-born criminal called John Palmer – who was later linked to handling the proceeds of some of the biggest heists of the 1980s – proudly boasted to his pals that he had at least a dozen police officers in his pocket.

Even while still in his teens, Palmer organised an illegal bare-knuckle boxing bout and 'employed' some local police officers to help keep the peace. 'These cops turned up in their uniforms and stood guard while the crowd went crazy and they got paid £20 each,' recalled one former Birmingham bank robber.

On another occasion, Palmer hosted a fight to the death between two notorious 'pikeys' (gypsies). The two men smashed each other to pieces for a £500 prize while more than ten times that amount changed hands in bets. The body of the loser was carried out of the makeshift ring by corrupt bobbies in their uniforms.

Palmer later claimed he paid those policemen for providing security with precious jewellery stolen earlier that very same day. The importance of 'greasing palms' was paramount to characters like John Palmer. As one of his oldest associates later recalled: 'Back then, we all had to pay backhanders to coppers at New Street nick (in Birmingham). Twenties here, tenners there and even nicked Tom (jewellery).'

The key to this street level of police corruption was that the criminals themselves needed to have police officers in their pocket so they could operate with impunity. Also, professional criminals back then believed policemen, judges and even politicians were all bribable characters who deserved no respect. Palmer later told one associate he liked moving from cop to cop because they always got too greedy. Some powerful criminals were collecting crooked policemen in much the same way other people collect vases or stamps.

One of the notorious gangster's favourite detectives at this time was an officer who later retired after years of 'feeding' Palmer information and then bought himself a country pile with the proceeds he'd 'earned' from the underworld. One of Palmer's oldest associates later told me: 'This old copper was shameless. He took tens of thousands, maybe even hundreds of thousands, off JP and others over many years and then he rubbed it in by buying himself a mansion and even got a big yacht.'

At one stage, the same crooked policeman offered to run Palmer and other villains back and forth from the Norfolk coast to Europe in his sixty-foot cruiser. This retired detective went on to become the go-to character for any gangster who wanted to travel in and out of Europe 'under the radar' for the following thirty years.

In later life, criminal mastermind Palmer ended up on the Spanish island of Tenerife, where he made tens of millions from a vast business of fraudulent time-shares. He later granted a newspaper interview during which he tried to expose some of the crooked police officers. Most believed it was a diversionary tactic to help hide some of his other criminal activities. When asked by the reporter if he missed England, Palmer replied: 'I miss England. I don't want to go into my personal life, I want you to help me bring this police corruption to task. I'm going to win. Then I'm going to sue every police officer that was involved.'

Back in the UK, meanwhile, some of Palmer's oldest police associates started to sit up and take notice because they didn't want their careers ruined by his indiscretions. *The Times* newspaper in London alleged that Palmer was protected for years by a 'clique' of high-ranking corrupt police officers who were themselves eventually exposed by a police probe.

Not long after this public outburst, John Palmer was shot dead by a hitman in the garden of his Essex home in June 2015. His murder has never been solved and there are rumours that a renegade gang of corrupt police officers either carried out the hit or paid someone else to do it for them.

There were even genuine fears that certain corrupt officers might try and hinder the investigation into Palmer's murder to protect themselves and their crime boss paymasters. Many said he had had it coming for years. But they also pointed out that whoever 'iced' Palmer would himself most likely be the underworld's next murder victim.

While Palmer paid the ultimate price for his involvement with police corruption, other criminals and their bent-copper associates switched to much less risky underworld enterprises.

TROUBLE IN GUNCHESTER

Manchester's reputation as an out-of-control city of crime was cemented during the early 1990s when there were so many firearms incidents that it was nicknamed 'Gunchester' in the media.

A number of old-fashioned crime families had staked a claim in the city's drug trade as violence exploded onto the streets, with shootings occurring virtually on a daily basis at one stage. Those crime families thrived because they had a string of high-ranking corrupt police officers acting as their eyes and ears inside Manchester's police force. And many of these infamous criminals and their tame coppers continue to operate inside the city even today.

Drug gangs and the police are still at loggerheads in the city. Behind the scenes, police and criminals continue to feed off each other, still fuelled by vast injections of cash earned through the lucrative drugs trade.

In some ways it's similar to how in 1970s London, the Flying Squad courted some of the capital's most notorious robbers and ended up in a sea of corruption and bribery that still reverberates in the UK capital today.

So it was with some trepidation and not a whole load of trust, I arranged to meet a recently retired Manchester detective aptly named 'Trouble' in one of the city's biggest cafes. The ex-detective has seen it all. He openly admitted to me he'd been thrown out of the police force after being accused of accepting a bribe. He made it sound as normal as directing traffic.

But Trouble insisted he'd been framed by his colleagues after having an affair with the wife of his married boss. He explained: 'Things work very differently here in Manchester from London. We never seemed to have enough time to devote to solving actual crimes. If a murder occurred here in the city, our bosses gave us a couple of days on the case and then insisted we give up and move on to other stuff.'

Trouble had been stationed in a district with a reputation as the so-called 'gateway' hub for drugs coming into Manchester. He shook his head as he recalled his time there. 'That was not a good time for me because many local gangsters did not like the way I focused all my energies on seeing what they were up to.'

Trouble believes he was then transferred out of that district after pressure was put on his boss by a group of corrupt Manchester detectives, who were on the payroll of local criminals. 'I stumbled on a drugs racket connected to three detectives who worked alongside me and that was like signing my own death warrant,' he told me.

That's how Trouble got his nickname: 'One criminal started calling me "Trouble" and it stuck.'

But Trouble's next posting inside the city was to an area of Manchester with a reputation for gun violence. Trouble admitted that during his six-month stay there, he was threatened 'many times' by drug barons operating in the surrounding areas. 'It was lawless there back then. I am a realist and if a gangster tells you to keep away from them in a place like that you do as they ask, otherwise they slit your throat.'

CRIME CITY

The city of Liverpool has always been run by old-school British gangsters, who've effectively sealed off the city's crime 'business' from the outside world. And a lot of their power and influence is down to corrupt police officers.

Series five of *Line of Duty* featured the ultimate ducking and diving crooked Scouser cop John Corbett. He is a superb character because in many ways he's a fine officer with an impressive track record. Yet he is driven by complicated domestic demons that have turned him crooked. And his Liverpool roots play a huge part in all this.

'Liverpool is a criminal state within a state,' explained one former Merseyside police officer. 'It's a tough place and it's always been run by its own underworld'.

Back in the 1990s, one legendary Liverpool born and bred so-called master criminal coined a chilling phrase that is still used in the city to this day:

'Bent coppers are the lifeblood of this city.'

As another retired Merseyside officer said: 'The big gangs expect the police to be corrupt here and unfortunately a number of my colleagues have been more than happy to oblige in the past.'

Veteran Liverpool criminal Dreads told me: 'Even our bent coppers stick to operating *only* inside the city. They know full well that if they started dealing with any villains outside the city, they'd soon be in deep shit.'

Liverpool's title of 'independent crime capital of Britain' has a lot to do with its port facilities, which have enabled local gangsters to buy drugs direct from the cartels in South America.

Dreads recalled: 'A couple of years back, some Albanian gangsters turned up here. They asked for a meeting with us in a local hotel. They said they wanted to use our port facilities to bring in some coke by ship from South America.

They promised us 60 per cent of the takings in exchange for those facilities.

'So we sent in a couple of our crooked coppers to meet them because we knew the Albanians wouldn't want any problems with the local police and they sent them packing.'

Then – on a side road out of the city – Liverpool gangsters made sure the Albanians got the message even more loud and clear. The Albanians' vehicles were stopped and local criminals lined them up against a wall and threatened to shoot them if they ever came back. They were never seen again.

One Albanian drug baron who operates in the south-east of England knows the gang of his fellow countrymen who tried to invade Liverpool. He told me: 'After that happened, our boys understood they had to stay away from Liverpool. I have to admit we were impressed that they even made us meet with their crooked cops.'

It seems that in many ways the Albanians respect the Liverpool gangsters immensely.

That same Albanian drug baron added: 'If a bunch of Liverpool gangsters tried to take over one of our cities back home, we would have done exactly the same thing.'

Many police and criminals admit that corrupt officers have helped these Liverpool gangs thrive in the city for many years. 'You need the boys in blue to be on your side in a place like this,' explained one local criminal. 'There's a tradition in these parts that the police will turn crooked if we treat them right.'

Liverpool criminal Dreads claimed that the police in the city have even encouraged the local underworld to stand up to the new foreign gangs. 'They didn't want what was happening across the rest of the country to happen here. At least we all know each other in this city. It makes life a lot easier.'

Another Liverpool criminal put it this way: 'A lot of this is also down to the city's infrastructure. We know every street here, especially in the areas near the docks. We've had spotter kids on every street corner in places like Toxteth since before many of those Albanians were even born.'

No wonder this city has been a law unto itself for more than fifty years.

Local criminal Dreads added: 'We've always cut out all the middlemen here, so no one can lean on us. We run every aspect of our produce [drugs] apart from the actual growing. We prefer it that way.'

Another Albanian drug lord who operates from the Midlands confirmed to me recently there were no plans to target Liverpool in the future. 'It's not worth it, we leave it to the Scousers. But one day someone will take them on and then maybe there will be a bloody war.'

One former city detective explained: 'This city's underworld thrives just beneath the surface. As a result, most normal people don't have a clue what's going on, except when something happens that affects them personally.'

BENEATH THE RADAR

The most tragic example of the impact on normal people was the murder of eleven-year-old Rhys Jones in August 2007. The youngster was caught in the crossfire between rival teenage drug gangs.

'That was extremely regrettable,' recalled one old-fashioned Liverpool gangster. 'I heard the Albanians thought we might be vulnerable after that happened and they had even considered trying to move in here but it came to nothing, luckily for them.'

But the murder of schoolboy Rhys Jones did have a serious knock-on effect as far as corrupt cops on the Liverpool underworld payroll were concerned. 'The city's criminals went into a lockdown after that kid was shot,' the same old-school gangster went on. 'The straight cops went berserk trying to find the killer of that poor kid and ended up stumbling on a number of crooked cops working for gangsters.'

The existence of renegade Liverpool police officers came as a great shock to many law-abiding citizens in the city. The local gangster continued: 'The police took a serious hit. Public confidence in them dive-bombed. Ironically, that left us with more "business" opportunities because many coppers were reluctant to steam in on us, in case we exposed them or their colleagues.'

However, Liverpool's underworld eventually fully recovered and over the past couple of years, recruitment of crooked officers has skyrocketed once again because the city continues to be such an important hub for drugs.

In early 2020, some of Liverpool's richest gangsters were rumoured to be planning to invest heavily in having the city's port facilities modernised through so-called legitimate construction businesses they either owned or had investments in. One recently retired Liverpool detective explained: 'There's a lot of villains here who want to turn Liverpool into a British version of Rotterdam, which is Europe's busiest port hub for drugs coming in from all over the world.'

As Liverpool gangster Dreads pointed out: 'If we're really going to turn this city into Rotterdam, we'll need even more corrupt coppers to help push this through.'

According to underworld sources in the city, some old-school renegade crooked cops are actually being paid commission by criminals to recruit more officers, so that they can consolidate control of all Liverpool's drug underworld. As one former Liverpool detective said: 'This place is turning into a mini narco state and there isn't much anyone can do about it.'

One local former bank robber explained: 'Many of the crime bosses know the local police because they often grew up together. Everyone knows everyone here. That means you always know when trouble is lurking. It also makes it a lot easier to tap up the local police. We know what pubs they drink in. We also know where they live.

'And let's face it. It's much better having a local born and bred copper on our tails because we can always turn that to our advantage.'

THE LAUNDROMAT

Line of Duty's anti-corruption team have not so far focused in on the most lucrative crime in the UK today – money laundering – and how it has helped fuel a modern-day epidemic of crooked police.

Numerous one-time UK drug barons have turned to

cleaning cash in recent years – often working for the mega-rich citizens of the nation's big cities. One very successful launderer explained: 'It's much less risky than dealing in drugs. And the police often struggle to get their head around laundering as a crime because it's not as clear-cut as other underworld enterprises.'

In an attempt to get a better handle on this, UK police recently recommended greater liaison between the police and tax authorities in order to keep watch on investments made by individuals or companies, many of whom do not pay either income or business tax, despite their operations being based in the UK.

Many real-life police investigators believe that the UK's billion-pound-plus cash-cleaning underworld has helped finance police corruption more than anything else in this country in recent years. Put simply, there is so much money involved with these nefarious activities that paying bribes to the police is considered a 'tax' by some mega-wealthy criminals.

And there is one nationality that dominates UK money laundering and pays out fortunes to those corrupt police officers.

THE RUSSIANS

The Russian mafia – who come mainly from Moscow and St Petersburg – have made big inroads into the UK in recent years. They're involved in fraud, drug trafficking, bribery, possessing firearms, and falsifying passports and credit cards.

But money laundering is at the centre of it all. As a result, the Russian criminals operating in this country have access to dozens of corrupt UK police officers, who often pull strings for their criminal enterprises. One London underworld source told me: 'The Russian gangsters in the UK are on another level. They have many corrupt UK policemen on tap at any time they wish to use them. Some of these bent coppers are being paid a monthly retainer of many thousands of pounds just to be on call for the Russians.

'The Russians themselves say it's now easier to bribe a police officer here in London than Moscow and it's much safer! Apparently, crooked cops in Russia bleed you dry of cash and then try to kill you to make sure you don't spill the beans about them.'

One former London detective explained: 'The Russians are cold as ice and wouldn't hesitate to kill you if they felt the need, especially in London. Money laundering is driving it all and it's the hardest crime of all to prevent. There are so many billions of pounds and dollars involved that no one would dare turn informant to the police. They wouldn't last five minutes.'

No wonder, then, that the relationship between these Russian gangsters and some of their crooked police associates can turn sour.

BLOOD RUNNING COLD

Often real-life police corruption is so subtle that it's virtually invisible to everyone apart from the people actually involved in it. Only a handful of people know that crooked cops played a chilling role in the death of a billionaire Russian criminal in 2015 at his huge mansion in the Home Counties on the edge of London.

The man's blubbery, naked body was found slumped on the ice-cold Italian marble floor of his bathroom. He appeared to have taken his own life. His head was slumped forward on his chest just like the thoughtful academic that he had once been, considering the intricacies of his navel. His face, umbilically inclined, was swollen and cyanosed: the lips were everted like small purple chipolatas, the dark staring eyes sightless and fixed, the white eyeballs haemorrhaging into streaks of scarlet. Around the angled neck was a constriction, a ligature unusual in that it was made from rope and torn sheets, which had cut deep into the throat.

The bathroom door was eventually forced open by his trusted bodyguard – a retired, UK police officer. He looked down at his boss momentarily, before testing the limp wrist for a pulse, knowing full well he wouldn't find one. Then he moved calmly towards a cupboard next to the body, took out a grey blanket and laid it carefully over the corpse.

Moments later, this same former London police officer quietly unlocked the door to a small office on the floor below and entered. He quickly found a black leather blotting-pad and calmly removed a see-through file from it that contained names and details of corrupt police officers on his boss's payroll.

An hour later, the corpse was lifted by two coroner's officers onto a gurney containing an open body bag, which was then carefully zipped up. Alongside them, two British MI5 officers in dark suits reminded the medical examiners that a full autopsy would need to be performed. By this time the victim's former police officer bodyguard was nowhere to be seen.

British security agents and police later told me this Russian crime boss was most likely the latest victim of a bloody secret war between him, his billionaire money-laundering partners and some of London's most corrupt police officers.

The bent cops were angry with the victim because he'd refused to pay them money owed to them for keeping him informed about allegations that Vladimir Putin's 'people' were planning to visit the UK to 'take care' of him.

When the stakes are high, the punishments will reflect that.

But why do so many corrupt police officers end up becoming private security or investigators?

ROGUE PIs

Line of Duty hasn't so far featured any storylines revolving around police officers who became private investigators. But in the real world, there are numerous such characters who often act as the buffers between serving officers and criminals. And a number of those private investigators have been linked to murder and corruption allegations in recent decades.

In 2013, Scotland Yard faced allegations that senior officers had for years ignored evidence that rogue private investigators had compromised the police service's highly sensitive witness-protection programme. It was claimed that PIs had been employed by organised crime gangs to find and then intimidate witnesses, who'd agreed to give evidence in high-profile court cases. They were also said to be bribing their former colleagues for information.

Those 2013 allegations were provided by a registered police informant codenamed 'Michael Green', who spent years working undercover with a corrupt private investigation company. He warned his handlers at the Metropolitan Police that the company were trying to locate 'supergrasses' under police protection with the sole intention of getting them to withdraw their evidence in upcoming trials or, worse still, have them killed.

The police are also alleged to have taken no action against the police officers-turned-private investigators who worked as phone hackers for the *News of the World* tabloid newspaper before it was closed down by press baron Rupert Murdoch in 2011, following the UK phone hacking scandal. One recently retired detective explained: 'A lot of officers suspected these claims were true but instead of arresting anyone, the whole thing was quietly swept under the carpet.'

In *Line of Duty*, senior police officers constantly put AC-12 chief Ted Hastings under pressure to stamp out corruption. But in real life, it seems many police commissioners across the UK have done little to tackle the sort of endemic, wholescale corruption highlighted throughout this book.

Another retired detective said: 'So many real-life versions of AC-12 have been set up over the past fifty years, but they never seem to have enough teeth to make a real dent on corruption and we know that former police officers who've become private investigators are at the centre of many allegations. But so many old-fashioned officers still refuse to believe corruption even exists in the first place. They fight tooth and nail to stop anti-corruption units from having any power and some of those old-school officers hold senior posts across the country.'

So why have so many high-profile police anti-corruption operations failed to stamp it out?

OPERATION COUNTRYMAN

Boldly announced police operations to crack down on corrupt officers have come and gone with alarming regularity in the real world, away from TV's *Line of Duty*. There have been numerous high-profile inquiries over the past forty years and none of them have achieved their objective because police corruption shows no real sign of being crushed.

In *Line of Duty*, it's the job of AC-12 to expose the bad cops, and in order to do so, the unit has to risk life and limb. Many detectives say that is exactly how it should be in real life too. But unlike the twisting and turning plots of the TV drama series, it can take many, many years for corrupt police officers to even start to be exposed.

Operation Countryman is a classic example. This highly publicised 1978–82 police investigation was supposed to clean up Scotland Yard's corruption problems, which had tainted the police so comprehensively throughout much of the previous two decades. It was codenamed 'Countryman' because of its use of officers from the so-called 'rural' police forces of Hampshire and Dorset, who would be less easily influenced by officers inside Scotland Yard.

Ordered by then Home Secretary Merlyn Rees, the Countryman investigation began by examining police activity around three extraordinary allegations that detectives in London had been involved in a 1977 robbery at the *Daily Mirror* newspaper offices in Holborn Circus, during which a guard had been killed and £200,000 stolen. Officers were also alleged to have connections to an earlier payroll snatch at the *Daily Express* offices in nearby Fleet Street during which £175,000 was stolen. Then there was a £225,000 robbery at Williams & Glyn's Bank in the City, also in 1977.

But crucial documents from Operation Countryman were not actually made public until 2018 – and that was only thanks to the efforts of one solitary police officer. DCS Steve Whitby served on the original investigation and had kept crucial papers back because he was so disgusted by what he saw as a police cover-up. Whitby was convinced officers had deliberately prevented the true scale of police corruption from ever coming to light back when the report was published nearly forty years earlier.

Following DCS Whitby's death in 2018, his family came forward to reveal his secret paperwork. It clearly showed how Whitby and his colleagues were thwarted by senior police officers and the then Director of Public Prosecutions (DPP). As one of DCS Whitby's family members recently told a newspaper: 'He felt peeved that individuals were allowed to get off scot-free. I did not want it to go to the rubbish tip without something being said or done.'

Operation Countryman was supposed to be investigating allegations against eighty-four members of the Metropolitan police and twenty-nine officers from the City of London police. They'd been accused of taking bribes, planting evidence, conspiring with bank robbers and improperly facilitating bail.

But Countryman itself resulted in just two successful prosecutions, much to the frustration and anger of investigators, including DCS Whitby, who'd been recruited from Dorset constabulary to join the investigation. He and other officers running the Countryman team had even been nicknamed 'The Swedey', a pun on the Flying Squad's nickname and for the fact they were regarded by the Met and City of London officers as being naïve, rural plods. They even designed a squad tie featuring a country mouse giving a V-sign to a hovering eagle, the Flying Squad's symbol.

Nevertheless, more and more secret documents from the operation came to light, thanks to DCS Whitby's efforts. They highlighted how successful attempts were made to force Countryman police officers including Whitby to pretend that London's Metropolitan Police had co-operated fully with them when the report was published all those years earlier.

'Operation Countryman actually put back the fight against police corruption by about twenty years,' said one retired London detective. 'We all knew it was a put-up job but no one seemed prepared to challenge it.'

When the investigation was over, Dorset Chief Constable Arthur Hambleton publicly stated he was 'absolutely staggered' by the extent of institutional corruption at Scotland Yard. He alleged that the then Director of Public

Prosecutions, Sir Thomas Hetherington – who died in 2007 – and some of Scotland Yard's highest-ranking officers had been obstructive. 'We felt the Director's office was never really with us,' he said after the collapse of the operation.

There were two key figures at the heart of the Countryman investigation: Alf Sheppard, a bank robber who was prepared to be wired to get evidence against corrupt officers, and a City of London officer, who was one of just two men later jailed. The same officer told Countryman investigators he first became involved in corrupt deals during his secondment to the Yard's regional crime squad, back in the mid-1970s. He said that it was a way of life and involved deals, informants, money and recovered property. Any reluctance to participate resulted in the officer being forced to leave the squad.

The Countryman inquiry team were told by one witness that a serving detective received £20,000 for allowing bail during a robbery investigation. That witness died in 1993 after denying making the claim, saying he'd been drunk at the time he made the allegation.

Crucially, the Countryman inquiry team were refused permission to grant immunity to criminals prepared to give evidence of police corruption. This effectively killed off their chances of bringing all the bad cops to justice.

As is clear from watching *Line of Duty*, police officers are not always there to protect and serve. And it was no different by the time the next big headline-hitting Scotland Yard operation to smoke out corrupt officers came in 2002.

TIBERIUS

Operation Tiberius identified eight criminal networks involved in drug trafficking, extortion and money laundering that were being helped by forty-two named serving and twenty-two former Metropolitan Police detectives. But media coverage was kept to a minimum because – it was later claimed – senior officers managed to bury the report.

Tiberius had originally been launched in 2001 after an internal probe found several investigations into organised crime had been compromised by the involvement of known corrupt police officers. Criminals including a notorious London crime family and drug gangs were said to have police officers on their payroll who were connected to a recently murdered former robber, money launderer and gold bullion smelter.

The confidential report recommended the UK's police should be cleaned up by a new task force created to investigate both organised crime and its connections to police corruption, but retired London police detectives I've spoken to ended up disillusioned when the unit was never set up. Instead, most officers suspected of corruption were allowed to resign or moved to different departments rather than be prosecuted or disciplined.

A former senior detective who investigated the syndicates said: 'This report exposed corrupt networks but what did they do with it? It was buried. Most of these organised crime groups are still operating today. Clearly the government had no real appetite for exposing corrupting officers.'

There were even allegations in the same report that details

of police investigations into at least five unsolved gangland murders had been leaked to actual suspects by corrupt officers. Many of them remained in senior posts for a number of years, despite being investigated by Operation Tiberius investigators.

One former south London detective explained: 'The top brass buried everything that Operation Tiberius tried to expose. That's a cover-up in itself. How could we have claimed back then to be cleaning this all up if we weren't even prepared to bring the bad guys to justice?'

At the time of writing, there had still been no attempt whatsoever by senior police to explain why the recommendations in the Tiberius probe were ignored. It would be more than ten years until another team of investigators was formed to look more closely at UK police corruption. And yet again, few believed such an operation would ever stop the rot.

OPERATION EMBLEY

The fallout from the Operation Countryman and Tiberius 'whitewashes' was a long time coming. But in the end, it did have the knock-on effect of forcing UK police to finally set up yet another inquiry into corruption. This time it was called Operation Embley.

Embley's breakthrough in 2018 came when the Independent Office for Police Conduct (IOPC) received tips from three officers that the Directorate of Professional Standards (DPS) had protected officers who faced allegations of child abuse, fraud, physical assault and racism.

Operation Embley evolved into the largest police corruption inquiry since Countryman in the 1970s. Yet following the investigation, none of the Scotland Yard officers being investigated were suspended from work and four others continued working inside the Yard's DPS anti-corruption unit on restricted duties. One officer had retired and another three were moved to other departments, though not as a result of the investigation.

In May 2019, eight officers and one member of staff belonging to the DPS were put under investigation for abusing their positions to unduly influence the ongoing Operation Embley investigation. By this time, the investigation was focusing on twenty-one allegations of misconduct relating to twenty-five internal investigations at Scotland Yard. The officers being investigated ranged in rank from chief inspector to chief superintendent.

The allegations in Operation Embley included interfering in investigations to lower the severity of charges against an officer, assisting an officer accused of wrongdoing despite a conflict of interest, failing to properly engage with evidence and abuse of process while conducting an investigation, and dropping an allegation of racist behaviour in order to protect the reputation of Scotland Yard.

'We reviewed a great deal of material, which initially included over five million emails, along with statements given by the individuals concerned and are making good progress to concluding our investigation,' Steve Noonan, Director of the IOPC, stated in 2019.

'With a number of final investigation reports currently

being written,' added Noonan, 'we are also considering the culture, disciplinary processes and systems used by the DPS, to identify any relevant learning that will help the MPS improve their handling of internal investigations, giving confidence to the public and serving officers and police staff.'

At the time of writing, the fate of those officers and the final conclusions of Operation Embley were not expected to be made public until the end of 2020 at the earliest.

Line of Duty hasn't really highlighted the full extent of the risks facing any police officer who makes a statement accusing a colleague of being a crooked cop. But in real life, these types of informants can find themselves in extreme danger.

Chapter Four

BIG FISH

'This department's been watertight for years, fella, and now we're leaking like a colander!'

DCS Ted Hastings in *Line of Duty*

GREENO

Line of Duty is very much a contemporary TV drama containing characters that we come to know and love and sometimes even hate. A lot of this is down to the fact we can relate to them and their everyday problems. But, as we've already seen, back in the 1940s, policing was obviously a very different kettle of fish. For starters, there were no anti-corruption units looking into bent coppers.

Enter Chief Superintendent Ted Greeno. In some ways he was like a twisted, real-life urban version of Foyle, the popular UK TV police detective who operated on the coast of south-east England during the Second World War at a time when corruption played second fiddle to Hitler.

In some ways, *Line of Duty*'s AC-12 boss Ted Hastings resembles a modern-day version of Ted Greeno. They both appreciate the so-called grey areas of policing. Hastings' own background in trouble-torn Northern Ireland undoubtedly helped shape his entire attitude towards The Job in much the same way the war years affected Greeno.

Also, just like Greeno, Ted Hastings does things *his* way and *his* way *only*.

Greeno lived in a copper's netherworld, thanks to character traits that in many ways combined the wit of *Morse* with the gritty realism of Jack Regan in *The Sweeney* plus a sprinkling of *Inspector Frost*. The career of this legendary Scotland Yard detective peaked during an era when coppers and villains lived in each other's pockets. It was simply a different world.

But in fairness, there was at least a measure of respect from both sides back then. The politically correct obsessions of today were often ignored, and some reckon that police officers had more heart and soul back then than the diligent, workaholic contemporary detectives of *Line of Duty*.

In many ways, characters like Ted Greeno were a throwback. His band of officers and even many of the villains they pursued seem to have an olde worlde charm to them, even though Greeno himself wasn't averse to turning a blind eye to corruption.

His career spanned from the twenties to the late fifties, but he was at his peak in London during the war. It was a unique policing era, with the dramatic background of the Blitz and a thriving black market, that, as we've seen, has since been blamed for helping to turn Britain into a nation of spivs and petty thieves.

Many of the cases handled by Greeno came about because the nation was at war and there was a gross shortage of police officers in the capital. Few people realised that, as a result, the murder rate rose by 70 per cent between 1939 and 1945. Crime itself is said to have doubled.

During this period, Greeno was one of the so-called feared 'Big Five' of London's top policemen. He had a quarter of all Greater London's CID under his command yet his salary was less than £2,000 a year (equivalent to about £25,000 today).

As Greeno himself later said: 'But fortunately, I could win that in a week at the races. When Pearl Diver won the Derby, I cleared £5,000. Maybe I should have banked it all, but I spent the cash in places that crooks can ill afford. I spent money in quieter places, too, and I got information.'

In other words, he often used his winnings on the horses to pay informants.

It seems incredible that a senior police officer would openly admit to an addiction to gambling without fearing the sack at the very least. And many veteran officers believe to this day that Greeno made himself vulnerable to actual corruption through his out-of-control gambling habits. As one retired detective explained: 'These days he would have been dubbed bent and either kicked out of the force or worse still, nicked for corruption.'

There is no doubt that Greeno encouraged his own Flying Squad detectives to nurture criminals as informants. These days, even these sorts of practices are frowned upon because they so often lead to corruption.

Greeno himself had a unique take on villains and prided himself on his ability to infiltrate the underworld. He used many of his longstanding criminal contacts to help solve brutal, shocking murders that hit the headlines at the time.

But did he use straight or crooked means to bring the bad guys to justice?

THE GREY AREA

Greeno wrote a bestselling autobiography after he retired. In *War On The Underworld* (published in 1960), he proudly re-emphasised his love of gambling:

'I've been catching criminals for thirty-eight years and backing horses for thirty-nine. If I had not backed so many winners, I could not have caught so many criminals, because at both sports you need information, which costs money.'

However, rumours of Greeno's own corrupt practices would end up haunting him until the day he died. Publication of his book certainly didn't help, either.

One expert on Scotland Yard later explained: 'Greeno helped set up the climate of corruption that poisoned policing from the 1960s through to at least the 1990s. That doesn't mean he himself was definitely crooked, but he believed in that grey area which so many police officers inhabited back then. This enabled a lot of dodgy coppers to use their relationships with criminals in a corrupt manner.'

Greeno himself claimed to have a photographic memory

and prided himself on knowing everything about many of London's most notorious villains. As he later explained in his book: 'I got to know criminal faces until I had 10,000 or more card-indexed in this peculiar policeman's mind of mine.'

Greeno even excused his addiction to gambling on the basis that it helped him get close to many of London's best-known underworld bosses. When officials at Kempton Park racecourse tipped the police that a gang were about to flood Britain with forged stamps, bonds and fifty-dollar bills, Greeno was already on the case because it was one of his favourite racetracks and he was there enjoying a flutter on the 'gee-gees'.

But was he a crooked police officer?

STRONG-ARMED

In London's West End, Ted Greeno did a lot of what we would today call 'socialising' with criminals. He claimed this helped him to get regularly tipped off about crimes *before* they were even committed.

On one occasion, the Flying Squad went undercover in a plain-coloured Bedford van and arrested a group of East End pickpockets run by legendary London underworld king Jack Spot's old boss, Long Hymie. But some of Greeno's colleagues later claimed that Greeno often overlooked the behaviour of his criminal contacts in exchange for headline-hitting swoops and arrests.

Greeno's arrest record was indeed impressive, as he liked to point out to anyone prepared to listen: 'I've personally handled twelve top murder investigations and solved them all – and 100 per cent is even better than my record with Derby winners.'

Greeno was commended eighty-eight times by judges, magistrates and the Commissioners at Scotland Yard. In 1949, he was awarded an MBE.

Greeno summed up his own philosophy as thus: 'As to whether I was too rough with criminals, I was never rough for the sake of it, but when I saw trouble coming, I forestalled it. I have given some villains awful hidings. I think if more policemen showed more villains that it is not only the lawbreaker who has strong arms, we would be nearer the end of this age of violent nonsense.'

But the one thing that Greeno tried to avoid discussing was police corruption. He knew it was endemic but believed that some of his senior colleagues used the subject as a 'stick' with which to hit hard-working police officers. He knew many officers who'd taken a few backhanders while out on the beat to turn a blind eye. But that didn't matter to him if those same officers took lots of villains off the streets.

However, Ted Greeno was clearly a man of many sides. When he heard that a judge had been framed by two crooked Scotland Yard cops, so that notorious London gangster Billy Hill's gang could 'influence' criminal trials at the Old Bailey, he worked relentlessly to try and expose the bad guys.

One Scotland Yard historian explained: 'Greeno drew the line where he wanted it drawn. The trouble was that he often stepped over that line into areas that would be seen as downright corrupt these days.'

THE ESTABLISHMENT

Ted Greeno seriously underestimated the power of the Establishment. He was warned off exposing one crooked judge by his bosses and politicians, who refused to accept that their honourable friend was on the take.

When Greeno kept pressing, he was demoted to a desk job. It's been claimed that inside the Yard it was implied that Greeno himself was crooked as a convenient smokescreen to take attention away from the supposedly corrupt judge.

As one former Scotland Yard detective later told me: 'Greeno was hailed as one of the first coppers to try and tackle real corruption inside the force. He wanted to take down the corrupt senior officers, some of whom were his own bosses. But there were also rumours that he used all this as a smokescreen for his own corruption.'

Greeno's obsession with bringing down the Establishment meant that ultimately he failed to see that he was falling into multiple traps. The Establishment wanted him out of Scotland Yard, and implying he was corrupt undoubtedly helped them get rid of him.

A few years back, such characters in the police would have been described by colleagues and bosses as 'eccentric' or 'unusual'. No doubt some would have labelled Ted Hastings as 'selfish' and 'impetuous', too.

But do these character traits prevent an officer from being an effective police anti-corruption investigator?

BIFFO

In the real police world, I've encountered a couple of Ted Hastings 'types' over the past thirty years, but one of them really does stand out from the crowd. I first met Biffo when he was chief of detectives at a suburban police station in the area where I trained as a young journalist in the mid-1970s.

Most of the classic 'thief-catchers' of that era were flashy, gritty, often humourless characters. But Biffo was the complete opposite. He wore his heart on his sleeve. He was softly spoken, respectful to women, and prepared to talk in depth – and enjoy a pint – with the 'enemy', which was what journalists were considered by many police officers back then.

The one big difference between Biffo and Ted Hastings was that Biffo stayed married to one woman for his entire life. He once described her to me as 'my Rock of Gibraltar' and believed that without her by his side, he would never have survived thirty years in the police service.

Biffo was born and brought up in a tough south London neighbourhood. But his relaxed, laid-back manner was often mistaken for a corrupt attitude by some of his superiors. They also accused him of not taking his job seriously. 'Which was bollocks, of course,' Biffo told me. 'But I never crawled up to the top brass, so I think that unnerved them.'

There is no way Biffo was ever 'on the take'. And, just like Ted Hastings, he earned incredible loyalty from his detectives because he was always prepared to put himself on the line for them.

But there was another even more significant similarity

between Biffo and his fictional counterpart Ted Hastings. Biffo went on to be made head of an anti-corruption unit during a period in police history renowned for bent coppers.

'No one else wanted the fuckin' job,' he told me. 'But I saw it as a challenge and I knew the bosses would keep well away from me. Most of them hated my guts and wanted me to screw it up anyway.'

Like all good coppers, Biffo was brilliant at getting inside the heads of his colleagues and second-guessing his bosses. It's another thing he and Hastings have in common. 'I know when something's wrong instinctively,' said Biffo. 'But I don't get angry with people who lie to me. I keep it gentle and low-key and then they usually tell me the truth.'

But when it came to his officers, Biffo believed in trusting them just as Hastings does in *Line of Duty*. Biffo explained: 'You can't run an anti-corruption unit on fear. You all need to pull together if you're going to smoke out the bad apples. I can see a lot of me in Hastings. But he needs to watch his back even more than he does at the moment, because he'll be sacrificed if his superiors start getting twitchy.'

Nonetheless, Biffo did have one significant criticism of *Line of Duty*.

He said: 'Hastings makes it look too easy to find detectives to work for him at AC-12. In real life, it was much harder. Most ambitious coppers don't want to join an anti-corruption unit because they believe it will ruin their careers in the long term.

'And then there are some officers who clearly have ulterior motives for wanting to work inside such a unit. They might well be already corrupt and planted in an anti-corruption unit on behalf of their own corrupt bosses.'

After failing to recruit suitable staff for his unit, Biffo persuaded his bosses to allow him to hire officers from outside the force under a special agreement through two chief constables. 'I was trying to tell the rest of the force that my unit would pursue anyone, irrelevant of rank, if they were suspected of being corrupt. There would be no friends in high places for any of them.'

Biffo once exposed one of his own members of staff when he discovered the officer was reporting directly to a senior officer in another department, who was secretly monitoring the anti-corruption unit.

But the primary aim of Biffo's unit was to expose corrupt cops who were on the payroll of notorious criminals. And none came bigger or more powerful than Mickey Green.

THE PIMPERNEL

The role of *Line of Duty*'s recurring professional criminal character Tommy Hunter was spread over the drama's first three series and sparked murder and mayhem inside and outside AC-12.

But it was nothing compared to real-life bank robber and cocaine baron Mickey Green's connections to corrupt police in the UK and Western Europe during the 1980s and 1990s.

Green, from west London, virtually single-handedly changed the rules when it came to crooked cops by employing his own personal stable of corrupt officers to stay one step ahead of the law. This has undoubtedly enabled him to stay free to this day and helped earn him his underworld nickname 'The Pimpernel'. It's even alleged that he got corrupt detectives to frame his criminal rivals.

In the 1990s, Green – described from the mid-1980s onwards by UK and Eire lawmakers as one of the world's biggest cocaine traffickers – was released on a legal technicality in Spain after being arrested on suspicion of drug smuggling. Many believe he paid his way out of jail by bribing poorly paid Spanish police officers.

Green already had known links to the Italian Mafia and Colombian drug cartels. In the 1990s, he was a regular visitor to South America, where he pulled off a number of huge cocaine deals with the world's most dangerous drug baron, Pablo Escobar, who was later killed by drug-enforcement agents in Colombia in 1993.

Green had been entrusted with millions of pounds by two big London robbery gangs, who knew they could earn vast profits from cocaine if it was purchased direct from the 'source' in Colombia. Splashing out cash on drug deals was also a great way to launder the proceeds from those heists. Green took a 40 per cent cut of everything and he wasn't in the slightest bit fazed by travelling to places like Medellín in Colombia – a city ruled by Escobar and his drug cartel.

No wonder British, Dutch, French and US authorities – all of whom suspected Green of major criminal activities – shadowed him around the globe. There were even rumours he'd kept an emergency fund of £1 million in French francs hidden in a box buried under the flowerbed at his villa in Marbella on Spain's notorious Costa del Crime.

But it was Green's stable of tame UK police officers that most helped him keep one step ahead of his global law enforcement pursuers.

When American DEA agents monitoring drug barons in Colombia reported that a 'limey' criminal had been seen in a series of meetings with Pablo Escobar, they passed on Green's name and details to their colleagues at Scotland Yard. One source later told me: 'Mickey Green was immediately told by a corrupt copper that the DEA had given the Yard a photo of him in Colombia. He immediately pulled out of Medellín after telling Escobar about the DEA. Escobar was impressed that Green had such powerful cops on his payroll.'

At one stage, police officers in London deliberately kept their distance from Green in the hope that he might eventually lead them to the two gangs of robbers, who'd allowed him to invest the proceeds from their heists. A source later claimed that Green's corrupt senior police officers gave this order as a smokescreen to protect him.

From then on, Mickey Green stayed away from the UK. But he continued to pay his stable of corrupt London cops so as to keep one step ahead of the police across Europe and the Americas. By then he was spending most of his time at his vast detached hacienda in Spain, where local corrupt Policía Nacional officers had kept him in the loop.

Then in 2000, Green suddenly pulled out of Spain and completely disappeared. I was told by one of my main underworld contacts on the Costa del Sol that he headed to Thailand and then Costa Rica.

One retired detective – who encountered Green during

his heyday in the 1980s – later explained: 'Mickey played us all off against each other, knowing that his tame cops would protect him. Mickey once proudly told me he had some very senior coppers in his pocket. I didn't believe him at first, but Mickey's managed to avoid prison for more than twenty years – despite all his criminal activities – so I guess he was telling the truth.'

Another former detective who dealt with Mickey Green when he was a master robber on the streets of London in the 1970s is convinced Green had so much evidence of police corruption that he could have brought down many senior officers in the south-east of England. That made him untouchable as far as the police were concerned.

That same former detective said: 'Green used all that knowledge of police corruption to guarantee he could continue to operate as a criminal when he should have been brought to justice and locked away for a very long time. Maybe he's dead by now but whatever has happened to him, he's had a better time than if he'd been locked up in prison.'

Another of Mickey Green's oldest associates also earned himself the protection of corrupt law enforcement, but he was a much more reckless character, who courted danger wherever he went.

JOEY BOY

Many ruthless criminals emerged from the UK underworld in the second half of the last century, but gangster Joey Wilkins took police corruption to new heights.

Wilkins' underworld career spanned from the 1950s to just ten years ago. During that time he was a spy, pimp, bank robber, conman, gangster, drug runner, police informant and was even rumoured to be a contract killer. And all of these criminal activities were underpinned by corrupt law-enforcement officers.

Joey Wilkins' life of crime started when he was a hustler in sleazy Soho in the 1950s. Then he became a bank robber in the 1960s and 1970s. That's when he first started 'buying drinks' for police officers.

But Wilkins took his involvement with crooked cops to a new level when he played an informant's role in the shoot-to-kill deaths of three IRA terrorists on the Rock of Gibraltar in March 1988. He later admitted he provided information about the IRA's plans to a crooked detective he knew, who was trying to prove to his bosses that he wasn't corrupt. Wilkins had been told about the terror plan by an IRA drug baron contact on Spain's Costa del Crime.

One old-school bank robber later told me: 'Joey was the most manipulative person I have ever met. He could charm the birds off the trees but that stunt in Gibraltar really took the biscuit. He was in touch with a bent cop who was about to be busted by his bosses and he wanted something really big from Joey in order to convince his bosses that Joey was an important informant.

'Joey helped this cop to make sure he "owned" him for life. It made complete sense.'

Joey Wilkins' tip about the three IRA terrorists planning an attack in Gibraltar led directly to security services gunning down and killing those suspects on the British colony just hours before they were due to mount an attack on British services personnel.

'Joey was very proud of that one. He knew the IRA might not be so happy if they'd heard about his involvement, though. I don't know to this day if they knew he'd informed on them,' added the same professional criminal.

Wilkins continued living in the drug-riddled killing fields of southern Spain until the early 1990s. He remained untouchable by the authorities. Then he went back to London only to be arrested for drug offences. He got six years in prison and complained bitterly that his corrupt cops had failed to help him stay out of jail, despite his earlier tip about the IRA raid in Gibraltar.

From inside a UK jail, he then threatened to expose corrupt cops and a UK security service agent he'd dealt with during the IRA 'episode'. Wilkins told senior Scotland Yard investigators that he'd paid them all retainers. Artful Joey was trying to strike a 'deal'.

Shortly after this, he left prison one day under police escort to visit the dentist for some essential repair work. Outside the dental surgery, Wilkins ran off up a busy Sussex high street and disappeared into crowds of shoppers.

One of Wilkins' oldest criminal associates later explained: 'Joey negotiated his escape. The guards did nothing and let him do a runner. Joey had been assured no one would come after him because he knew where all the bodies were buried.'

Wilkins soon arrived back on his beloved Costa del Sol. Officially he was a wanted man but no attempt was ever made to re-arrest him. He later told friends and associates in Spain that he'd been given his freedom in exchange for his silence about police and security-services corruption.

Joey Wilkins died under mysterious circumstances in Spain in 2006. Some said it was a heart attack. Others claimed he'd been murdered. 'I reckon someone got him in the end,' said one of Wilkins' oldest friends, also a notorious professional criminal.

Joey Wilkins was certainly a one-off character. But more recently there have been some even more powerful 'faces', who've turned the tainted world of UK police corruption upside down.

COCKY

A real-life version of *Line of Duty*'s deeply flawed Liverpool cop John Corbett (played by award-winning actor Stephen Graham) would no doubt have known all about Curtis Warren, aka Cocky.

As he left the dock after being acquitted of drug charges one time, Cocky told customs officers: 'I'm off to spend my £87 million from the first shipment and you can't fuckin' touch me!'

He boasted to associates that his corrupt, mainly Liverpool police officers got handsomely rewarded for their unswerving loyalty after that case against him was thrown out. Cocky recognised that having police officers on his payroll was crucial to the success of his criminal empire.

In the mid-1990s, he teamed up with a drug baron based

in the north-east of England to give them both complete dominance of the English drug market north of Birmingham. These two characters pulled in so much cash that they became multi-millionaires virtually overnight.

And in the midst of all this, jealous small-time gangsters across Liverpool were constantly grassing up Cocky Warren's activities. But his answer was simply to recruit even more boys in blue. Amongst them was Merseyside Detective Chief Inspector Elmore Davies – later jailed for five years for corruption for his part in trying to get one of Cocky's acquaintances off a firearms charge.

In September 1991, Cocky climbed the global drugs ladder when he and his north-east drug-baron associate travelled from Dover to Calais by ferry on fake British visitor passports. Accompanying them was a 'marketing representative' for the Cali cartel in Colombia. Cocky also had another former Liverpool detective accompanying him as his personal bodyguard.

Cocky and his associates assured immigration officers they'd only be travelling inside Europe. Then they drove to Brussels airport, where they parked their car and caught a plane to Malaga, Spain. From Malaga, they went up to Madrid. Then Cocky and his accomplice took out their own genuine ten-year regular passports and flew across to Caracas, Venezuela, which just happens to share its border with Colombia.

In South America, Cocky was introduced to Camillo Jesus Ortiz, who headed up a company formed on behalf of the Colombian Cali cartel's front firm – the Conar Corporation. Cocky and his partner put down a £6 million deposit for two giant shipments of cocaine. The first – of 1.5 tonnes – would arrive in the port of Felixstowe the following month, October 1991. The coke would be hidden in steel boxes sealed inside lead ingots, which were not easy to slice open and impossible to X-ray. Cocky would have two corrupt cops on hand to ensure the shipment got through.

Just before it was due to arrive, Cocky flew to Amsterdam with his ex-cop bodyguard and two associates, Anthony Cahill and Colin Smith, to discuss the final details of the deal with the Colombians. Within days, Cocky and his team were informed their goods were on the way from South America and he awaited the shipment from Felixstowe.

Cocky eventually arrived with special tools to remove 500 kg of cocaine, which he would then distribute in Britain, while the rest went on to the Netherlands and Greece. His distribution deal guaranteed he was already in profit before he'd even flogged a gram of his coke on Merseyside.

And Cocky's personal 'team' of crooked cops continued to play a pivotal role in it all.

One former Liverpool detective explained: 'Cocky was clever in that he made sure a lot of his bent coppers joined him on actual dealings with the Colombians. That meant they couldn't wriggle out of involvement. They were completely incriminated, just the way Cocky wanted.'

When one later shipment of cocaine left Felixstowe, Dutch police tipped off British customs that a major shipment of drugs was hidden in steel boxes inside lead ingots. Customs even cut open one ingot in the shipment from South America but found nothing. The ingots were released and taken to a warehouse outside Liverpool. A senior Colombian cartel member was on site to extract the cocaine. The ingots were then buried in rubble at a mill before being sold for scrap, ending up in Newcastle.

Another shipment containing 900 kg of cocaine left Venezuela in December that year. As it came in, Cocky and his main henchmen were arrested. It looked as if the long arm of the law had finally caught up with them.

But then certain police officers – whose real identities have never been disclosed – came forward and claimed Cocky's henchman was an informant and should be allowed to walk free so that he could put the finger on some even bigger fish.

It's alleged that corrupt police officers then deliberately wrecked the prosecutor's case against Cocky and his crew. The henchman was released and the case against him at Newcastle Crown Court collapsed in 1992.

Cocky's acquittal in Newcastle sent a message to the cartels he dealt with in South America. They now knew that – although Cocky had faced decades in prison if convicted – he would always keep his mouth shut. He'd never once offered to inform on the Colombians. This was a man to be trusted. And the fact he also had the police in his pocket was even further proof that Cocky Warren was a man to do business with.

Not surprisingly, though, law-abiding police remained determined to bring Cocky to justice. They were appalled that he seemed to have so many crooked detectives on his payroll.

Less than six months later, customs officers conducted a covert search of a lorry at the Suffolk port of Felixstowe and found 250 kg of heroin. They watched as it was driven to Burton Wood services on the M62 near Liverpool. Then Cocky drove into the compound. But he spotted the police surveillance officers and scarpered. He had already been told by one of the crooked cops on his payroll that the police would be there and he was simply 'testing them' by driving into the compound and then driving straight out again.

As a result of this, UK Customs launched Operation Crayfish to try and catch Cocky. He was to get twenty-four-hour round-the-clock surveillance with 'all the trimmings'. However, having a unit of corrupt Liverpool cops in his pocket helped him stay one step ahead of the authorities.

Eventually Dutch police monitoring Cocky's phones tipped off Merseyside police about a drug shipment. They'd planted a camera in Warren's friend's flat, which they hoped would also help them gather enough evidence to bring about a successful prosecution of any crooked coppers working for him.

But it never happened and many in Liverpool believe that Cocky Warren knew all about the police surveillance operation, thanks to the crooked cops on his payroll. By this time, the criminal was shelling out hundreds of thousands of pounds in bribes to crooked Merseyside officers.

The long arm of the law only finally caught up with Cocky Warren in the late 1990s when he was imprisoned on multiple charges. It's rumoured that he was finally released from prison in early 2020. Many inside the Liverpool underworld believe that his return to the city could well spark a gang war like no other with numerous corrupt police officers at the centre of it.

Curtis 'Cocky' Warren was said by many to be a born criminal, but is there such a thing as a 'born corrupt cop'?

TRIGGER

I've encountered numerous bent coppers over the past thirty years but probably the most unusual was a character we'll call Trigger, whom I first interviewed more than twenty years ago on southern Spain's notorious Costa del Crime.

Not even the fertile imagination of *Line of Duty* creator Jed Mercurio could come up with such a bizarre, twisted and dangerous character as Trigger.

He was thrown out of the UK police force in the 1990s for alleged corruption, although he always insisted it was never proven. Trigger left the police with little fanfare because – like so many corrupt cops – his bosses did not want him shouting it all from the rooftops, so they let him 'retire' despite a litany of corruption allegations against him.

Trigger claimed many of his superior officers spent years after his exit from the police worried that he might bring them down. 'I'm fuckin' surprised I'm still alive,' Trigger said to me cheerfully one sunny day in Marbella a few years ago. 'You could call me a dead man walking if you want, but they ain't got me yet!'

And despite his modest police salary, Trigger had all the classic trappings of wealth by the time we met. In fact, a combination of payoffs from criminals and his own dodgy businesses seemed to have made him a fortune.

When we first met in the early 2000s, Trigger owned a

nightclub near Marbella, which was mainly frequented by prostitutes and criminals. Many of those villains were 'new arrivals' from Russia, which had been 'exporting' oligarchs and gangsters from St Petersburg and Moscow since the collapse of communism. 'I'm not a pimp,' he explained. 'I don't take any cash off those girls. What they do with the customers is up to them. I just provide a place for them all to get together.'

He never hid his UK police background from anyone. He told me: 'A lot of the villains who come to my club love the fact I used to be a copper. I don't hide it because it's better than them finding out from someone else. Keeping it in plain sight is definitely the way to go.'

He had 'acquired' the club a few years earlier thanks to a drug debt owed to him by a gang of Spanish gangsters who operated in a town called La Línea, opposite the British colony of Gibraltar. La Línea is probably the nearest thing to a 'narco city' in all of Spain.

Trigger had already been married and divorced four times by the time we met and was living in a flat next to the club with a Moroccan woman thirty years his junior.

He said: 'Most of my old copper mates think I'm scum but I don't care about that. Remember, I know more about police corruption than most of them and it's helped me survive.'

In 2012, two serving detectives from Scotland Yard visited Trigger's club to interview him as part of an ongoing anti-corruption operation back in the UK. 'I was polite to them but I told them nothing because I don't want to be responsible for nailing another copper,' he said. 'I know what it's like. It's just not my style. Listen, I'm just quietly getting on with my various businesses interests here, so the last thing I want is to be dragged into a fucking bent cop inquiry.'

However, Trigger's calm exterior hid a very volatile personality. Only a few weeks before we last met, he'd been thrown half out of a car and dragged one hundred metres along a nearby carreterra (motorway) after falling out with two Russians. They'd wanted him to set up the purchase of a large load of cocaine from a Colombian cartel based near Malaga.

Scratching a deep scar across the side of his forehead, Trigger later recalled: 'I got this, thanks to those two bastards. They thought that if they roughed me up, I'd put them in touch with the Colombians. But I didn't trust them and the Colombians would have come back at me if those two Russians had turned out to be Feds [police].'

Trigger's reign on the Costa del Crime was also constantly under threat at this time from the Guardia Civil Spanish police force, many of whom detested him. He explained: 'I've got two corrupt Marbella cops from the local Policía Nacional on my payroll, but they often let me down and I end up getting raided.

'One time, three van loads of Guardia Civil turned up at my club, claiming I was running it as a brothel. They hate the Policía Nacional, so decided to pay me a visit. Some bastard gangster down here grassed me up because I'd chucked him out of the club a few nights earlier.'

Trigger claimed that in order to get the Spanish police

to drop charges against him, he had to pay them off, plus a corrupt officer back in the UK whom he knew 'from the bad old days'.

He explained: 'That Brit officer knew the Spanish cops who nicked me and he sorted it out for a few bob. But it says it all that there are still bent coppers back in the UK whom I can bribe. You'd think they would avoid me, wouldn't you?'

A couple of years back, Trigger and I discussed the first two series of *Line of Duty* in great detail and he gave me his verdict: 'I love that show. It makes me feel a whole lot better about what I got up to. It sometimes feels as if the writers are trying to turn all those bent coppers into heroes. Let me tell you, in the real world once the anti-corruption boys have you in their sights, you're in big shit.'

He went on: 'But in some ways the makers of *Line of Duty* have let the real police off the hook. On the programme, they're always trying to show the human side of even the most nasty coppers. But fully bent coppers have the empathy of a newt. I know because I was one once.'

The last time I saw Trigger was just before the third series of *Line of Duty* was about to be aired. We met in a bar just east of Marbella but he seemed a lot more downbeat than he'd previously been. 'I'm being leaned on by some really heavy characters down here,' he explained. 'I owe them money on a coke deal and they aren't going to let it ride.'

Trigger even asked me if I could lend him ten thousand pounds. I politely declined. He seemed bitterly disappointed.

A few days later, I tried to call Trigger but his mobile phone was coming up as unobtainable. Not long after that I bumped into another former police officer based on the Costa del Sol and asked him about Trigger.

'He's disappeared off the face of the earth, mate,' said the retired detective. 'You know what he's like. He's been ducking and diving for so long, maybe it's all finally caught up with him.'

From the tone of this man's voice, he clearly didn't like the man. Then I interviewed one of Trigger's friends in Marbella and he said Trigger had headed for El Salvador in Central America, after being tipped off by corrupt Spanish police that he was about to be arrested.

I never heard from Trigger again but there were rumours on the Costa del Crime that the Colombian cartel he owed money to had finally run out of patience.

Back in the UK, the 'business' of police corruption continues to thrive.

TANK

In *Line of Duty*, the standout classic old-school professional criminal is without doubt Tommy Hunter. He veers in and out of storylines for the first three series before 'departing'.

Hunter is a ruthless Scottish ganglord, who has his finger in many pies and – like so many similar real-life villains – he believed he would always come out on top, even against the police and security services. But that confidence was helped greatly by the knowledge that he had renegade corrupt police officers on his 'books'.

In the real world, I've met many Tommy Hunter-type

criminals. They're charming on the surface, although you can usually spot the ruthlessness in their soulless, dead eyes that snap around in all directions, constantly checking for trouble.

In late 2019, I was approached by a gangster who'd worked for one of the UK's most notorious crime families. He wanted to tell his story because he believed he'd be safer if he went public about his life inside the UK underworld.

But it wasn't just other criminals this gangster was scared of. He believed that a group of renegade crooked detectives were shadowing him on behalf of his onetime crime family bosses, who'd already tried to kill him in an attack a few years previously.

I've given this man a false name – Tank – because I know as well as him that the crime family would come after him if they knew he'd talked to me. They'd already put the word out throughout the south-east England underworld that Tank was a police informant, something he has always strenuously denied.

Tank insisted to me that the family member who'd tried to have him killed some years previously had actually himself been a police grass for more than twenty years. Tank explained: 'He targeted me because his bent copper mates wanted me out of the way, in case I grassed them up.'

My first clandestine meeting with Tank could have come straight out of *Line of Duty*.

We pulled our vehicles up next to each other in a deserted car park in the heart of the badlands of south-east England. It was close to the M25 motorway that encircles London and has played a pivotal role in so many notorious getaways by criminals since it was opened nearly forty years ago.

Tank had approached me after reading one of my books. He was desperate to unload everything he knew in case he ended up being murdered by the gang's renegade cops, whom he claimed were on his tail.

He revealed that the crooked detectives in question had been 'in the pocket' of this crime family for twenty years. 'They're so deeply in with the family that they couldn't get out, even if they wanted to,' explained Tank. 'I know they're after me. But those coppers are just waiting and watching me until they get the green light,' he added.

'I swear on my kids' lives that I've never been a police grass in my life,' he said, panning his eyes around the car park nervously as we sat in his vehicle.

When I pointed out that virtually every police informant I've ever met always says that, he laughed.

'I've watched *Line of Duty* and that's what they all say but that programme is a picnic compared to the real world,' said Tank. 'I've met coppers in recent years who're more dangerous and trigger-happy than anyone you'd ever see on that show.'

Tank is convinced that during the past decade – since *Line of Duty* first hit the small screen – corrupt cops have become even more daring and brazen. 'You'd think they'd watch their backs more, wouldn't you? But the series has made it almost glamorous to be bent. And they're getting even more greedy and reckless.

'A lot of it's down to the classic excuse: coppers' pay. They're falling behind most other jobs. Their wives and kids are demanding a lifestyle that many of them can't afford. As a result, they want their palms greased most of the time.'

Tank claimed that his crime-family bosses had corrupt officers spread across many police departments. 'They'd even let us know when other cozzers were getting themselves in trouble through drink, drugs and women. Then we'd pay 'em a visit and try and turn 'em crooked. Most of the time it worked.'

Tank revealed his unique insight into ongoing corrupt police activities to me only because he's convinced he will one day end up being killed on the orders of his former bosses. He explained: 'I'd already left the gang just before they shot me the first time. The family was in a meltdown because the real police were chasing them down harder than they'd ever experienced before. So they panicked and started looking around for people to blame for their problems and that's when they came after me. Saying I was a grass gave them an excuse.'

At one stage, Tank even agreed to a meeting with one family member so he could plead his innocence. 'I thought we was going to sort it all out man to man and then I could move on with my life,' he explained. 'But this was the same bastard I knew was a police informer. He'd already decided that if he did [kill] me then it would stop the rumours about him being bent and that would help him kill two birds with one stone, so to speak.

'By killing me, he could then be the hero who got rid of the grass. It nearly worked perfectly.'

Tank turned up for his meeting with the crime family member unaware of all this.

'We met in a lay-by of a busy A-road. I knew it'd be busy so he wouldn't dare take a pot-shot at me.'

But the two men then got into a heated argument.

'He started mouthing it off yet again about me being a grass. I was fuckin' furious. We was standing behind his car next to some bushes on the lay-by. Next thing I know, he's pointing a gun at me, aiming low towards my stomach in such a way that none of the cars driving by could have seen what he was doing.'

Moments later, Tank was shot once. He recalled: 'If he'd pumped another couple of bullets into me I would have been a goner, but after shooting just the once, he just jumped in his car and fucked off.'

Tank managed to clamber into his car and drive to the nearest hospital. The shooter was eventually arrested on various charges, including attempted murder.

'But that wasn't the end of it,' explained Tank. 'He got even more paranoid in prison and decided his bent coppers would do a better job than him, so he lined them up to finish me off. I heard he even wound them up into believing I was going to grass them up as well.'

Tank has been told by one associate who still works for the crime family that the renegade police unit working for them were originally due to kill him in the summer of 2019. 'But apparently it was called off because some real honest coppers were on my tail and the family and their crooked cops didn't want to get caught in the middle of it, so to speak,' he explained.

He has been told by his contact inside the crime family that the order for his execution will now stay on ice until the family member who shot him is released from prison. 'I've been told he [the family member] is so paranoid these days, he thinks the bent coppers might be undercover themselves, so he doesn't want to take the risk and press the button at the moment.'

These days, Tank describes himself as 'retired' and insisted to me that he doesn't need to commit any more crimes because he's got stashes of cash hidden all around south-east England: 'I'm out of the game completely and I intend to keep it that way.'

Tank claimed that he encountered at least a dozen corrupt police officers during the twenty years he worked with the crime family. 'Most of them were slimy, sneaky bastards. After all, they're stitching up their friends and their enemies at the same time.'

During his time with the family, he witnessed every side of police corruption first-hand. 'I've seen how bent officers are targeted and then manipulated by villains. Sometimes, the cops even came to us with their hands out, wanting paying. We'd pay 'em with cash, drugs, women... You name it.

'People like me and the family I used to work for know just how much pressure to put on those bent cops and believe me, we're not talking about a few lowly constables and sergeants here.'

But Tank insisted that none of the family's crooked stable of officers were ever paid enough money to give it all up and retire. As he explained: 'You don't want a bent cop just walking away from being crooked. You want them hanging on a string. It's the same as being a real villain in a sense.

'You can't just wake up one morning and decide "That's it, I'm off to my villa in the sun, where I'm going to enjoy a long and fruitful retirement." In yer dreams, mate! In yer dreams!'

WATCH YER BACK

Tank claimed that the crime family still have at least half a dozen 'tame' senior police officers inside police forces across the south-east of England, as well as lower-ranked officers whom they use for occasional 'favours'.

He said: 'When another member of the family got nicked by the cozzers when I was still working for them, he was allowed out on bail after I delivered a million quid in cash to the judge as "bail money"'.

Tank went on: 'I negotiated all that with one of this judge's clerks in the lay-by of a road on the south coast. The straight detectives who'd genuinely arrested this family member were fuckin' gutted when that villain got bail. Although I later heard that two of them had passed on the message to us that the judge was "buyable" in the first place.

'That's how it works with bent coppers. There's always one to help you out of trouble if you have the cash. It's wheels within wheels.'

But the relationship between Tank's crime family bosses and some of their corrupt officers took a very different turn recently. He explained: 'A couple of bent cops on the family payroll tried to turn the tables on them by arresting one of the family members. The family were well upset. Then these two coppers said they'd release the family member without charge if the family arranged for a contract killing to be carried out on a villain who'd upset those two bent cops.'

He went on: 'The family got the right hump over that, but they didn't have no choice. So two of the family members commissioned a freelance hitman from Albania we'd used in the past and gave him the job.'

It was only then that Tank and his associates inside the family discovered their target was actually a police officer, NOT a criminal.

Tank went on: 'We was outraged at first. But then one of the family members shrugged his shoulders and said we could use it to our advantage, so he arranged to get the job done. He reckoned those bent coppers would be like putty in our hands and he was right. We'd even secretly recorded our meetings with them and then let them know what we had, just in case they tried to stitch us up.'

Today, however, Tank no longer has the family's 'protection'. He told me: 'Now I've gotta watch me back every fuckin' minute of the day and night. I've got villains and bent coppers after me, it's doin' me head in.'

But Tank claimed he had some very 'fuckin' important' evidence hidden away, just in case the family do decide to finally silence him for ever: 'If they knock me off, I've got a system in place which will bring down every last one of them.'

As our conversation in his top-of-the-range SUV came to an end, two burly men approached the vehicle. Tank immediately looked up at them. 'Time to go,' he said, flicking on the engine as the men walked past, seemingly oblivious to us.

As I got out of the car, he leaned across and added, 'Hope to see you soon, mate.' And with that, he was gone.

I never heard from Tank again. My contacts in the south-east England underworld told me he'd 'gone to ground' after discovering that the crime family were on the verge of re-commissioning the renegade cops to kill him. The order had come from that family member inside his prison cell.

Tank never responded to any more of my calls and a few weeks after meeting him in that lay-by, his mobile phone was disconnected.

As Jerry – one of Tank's friends – later told me: 'He's disappeared. Maybe he's already six feet under or maybe he's got himself a new passport and headed off for the sunshine.'

Inside the police forces of the south-east, opinions of Tank are varied. One detective told me: 'He likes to puff himself up as the original gangster but he's not much more than a very average "soldier".'

Another officer said: 'Any copper who tells you that Tank is a nobody is probably batting for the other side [crooked] because in that world, they don't like to think that criminals have got the upper hand, so they demean them as much as possible.'

A few weeks after meeting Tank, a gangster known to him and many in the London underworld was gunned down in broad daylight on Spain's Costa del Sol.

One of my most reliable police sources told me: 'There's a rumour going round that Tank has either been killed by the same hitman or commissioned the job as a warning to the family's favourite corrupt coppers.'

What goes around comes around.

MICHAEL MICHAEL

One of the key skills for *Line of Duty*'s AC-12 police anti-corruption detectives is their ability to turn crooked police officers and criminals into informants in order to bring the most dangerous bent cops of all to justice. But in order to do that, investigators invariably need a two-timing crook like professional crime boss Tommy Hunter. These characters are manipulative, duplicitous and completely untrustworthy, but anti-corruption officers have to bite their lips and suffer them in order to nail down crooked cops.

Probably the most notorious real-life example of such a two-timing police informant was a criminal called Michael Michael – who in the 1980s was 'financial advisor' to a number of notorious professional criminals from south-east England.

Michael Michael was an accountant by trade and also helped run a string of massage parlours in the Home Counties with his common law wife, Lynn. Initially, he was arrested by police on suspicion of running a £3 million mortgage fraud, but it soon became clear to detectives that Michael was running a major crime organisation with links to many powerful members of the UK underworld.

They offered Michael a deal in exchange for a very lenient eight-month prison sentence. He became a registered, full-time police informant. Michael was even given the pseudonym Andrew Ridgeley, after the singing partner of George Michael, in the pop duo Wham!

Michael provided detectives with information about members of various criminal families and their activities in the UK and Spain to his police handler. He also blew the lid on numerous corrupt, mainly UK-based police officers.

Michael alleged he paid tens of thousands of pounds to bent cops on behalf of some of the most notorious professional criminals in Britain in exchange for information about other criminals and ongoing police investigations. Officers known to have gambling or drug problems were prime blackmail targets, who could then be 'turned' crooked.

I've seen copies of Michael Michael's official Scotland Yard contact sheets (forms filed by his police handler) and in them he also named numerous UK criminals dealing in drugs in Spain. Many of them also had tame police officers on their payroll, according to Michael.

He also admitted supervising the UK distribution of vast amounts of cannabis and cocaine, much of it smuggled into the UK from a transit point in southern Spain. Cannabis resin was hidden in drums suspended inside liquid tanker vehicles. Cocaine tended to be hidden in cars because it was much smaller in quantity. Some drugs were even stashed inside a secret compartment on a tourist coach, nicknamed the 'Magic Bus' after the song made famous by The Who.

Michael told police he regularly met with many of the UK's most notorious professional criminals in Spain, as well as at luxurious hotels in London's West End. He'd even laundered vast sums of money for them through a currency exchange bureau specifically set up in west London. He also explained how women were often hired as couriers to fly cash and drugs from Heathrow or Gatwick airport to Spain with two-week return tickets. But instead of staying, they usually returned the following day.

Michael revealed to detectives that he and his UK crime associates were happy to pay vast amounts of cash to crooked cops because it then meant they could later 'squeeze' them for information by reminding them that they had evidence of their corrupt practices.

He also told his police handler that a lot of confidential police information had also been filed away and then sold on to the highest bidder within the criminal under-world, if it was of no specific use to Michael and his crime bosses personally.

One former London detective explained: 'We were astounded by Michael Michael's statements. It seemed that corrupt officers were contributing to an information exchange business, literally. They were taking information from inside the police computer and selling it on to these criminals, who then sold the same info on to other villains.'

Michael Michael's exposé of this 'information business' being used to blackmail and coerce police officers shocked the top brass at Scotland Yard. It clearly implied that corruption had taken hold of certain departments inside the UK's premier crime fighting organisation.

As one detective later told me: 'This wasn't just a bit of help from a cop in exchange for a few bob under the table. The corrupt cops were selling negative information about their colleagues without caring what might happen to those officers. They'd been coerced by some of the most powerful criminals this country has ever seen.'

Not surprisingly, Michael Michael was given witness protection even while serving his original short sentence. This meant being kept in solitary confinement at all times for his own protection. 'There were very credible rumours that a gang of corrupt detectives had decided to take Michael out [kill him] on behalf of themselves and their criminal paymasters,' one retired London detective later told me.

Others inside the police tried to dismiss Michael Michael's claims by insisting he was making everything up in order to get a short prison sentence. However, another retired detective pointed out: 'But there was too much detail in what he was saying for it to have been made up.'

Criminals and police officers who met Michael at the time described him as being an 'extremely fearless individual'. One former detective said: 'He was the most amoral man I've ever met. He didn't even acknowledge that he was in any danger. He stayed in witness protection programme after he'd served his sentence because the police needed to keep him alive so he could give evidence.

'At first, I just thought Michael was a cold-hearted bastard but then it began to dawn on me that the reason he wasn't afraid was because what he'd told us was no more than the tip of the iceberg, literally.'

Detectives are now convinced that Michael only told them about 10 per cent of what he really knew about the underworld and police corruption because he wanted to dangle a carrot under their noses, so he could avoid a long prison sentence for his original offence.

The same detective explained: 'I believe that Michael's decision to be an informant was all pre-agreed with his criminal associates and corrupt police officers. It was a clever move if you think about it because he was able to appear to be helping the police when in fact he was actually protecting all the bad guys as well.'

These allegations gained weight a few months after Michael was released from his short prison sentence. Instead of setting up home with a new identity under witness protection, he began being seen out at his old London haunts.

As one detective later said: 'And guess what? No one even tried to take a pop at him. That's why so many of us are convinced he conned everyone with all that so-called evidence. I think he was encouraged to do it by villains who knew it would confuse the situation for the police.'

Michael Michael spent the next few months telling anyone who'd listen that he'd tricked the police and it had worked like a dream because he was now free and back in the outside world. But he was eventually hauled back into court to face new charges, including illegal possession of a firearm. This time he got a longer sentence of six years. After his eventual release from prison fifteen years ago, he promptly disappeared.

One retired London detective elaborates: 'I heard he was in Cyprus, living it up. If Michael had been killed, his body would have shown up because the sort of villains he was working with would have wanted his corpse to be found as a warning to others not to inform on them.'

So who were the corrupt officers Michael Michael exposed to the police but who then apparently slipped through the net?

KEL

Line of Duty has featured many female police officers in its storylines since series one first aired, back in 2011. Some officers have applauded this, while others have said it is an attempt by the programme makers to be politically correct.

Whatever the reasons, the activities of the programme's premier crooked lady cops Lindsay Denton and Roz Huntley pale into insignificance when compared with one real-life corrupt woman officer who slipped through the net around the time supergrass Michael Michael appeared to be singing like a canary.

We'll call her 'Kel', although she used to be referred to as 'that fuckin' woman cop' by some of south-east England's most notorious gangsters when she was a serving detective.

Kel belonged to a renegade syndicate of corrupt detectives in the 1990s, who planted evidence and framed criminals and even some of their own police colleagues. But she was never brought to justice, even after her activities were exposed by Michael Michael to some of London's most senior officers.

'Kel had them all by the balls,' one retired detective explained. 'If she'd publicly exposed what she'd been involved with then it could have brought down a lot of big names, so she was allowed to leave quietly.'

And Kel had big plans for a new career. She seamlessly immersed herself in the underworld of south-east England, where vicious Eastern European cartels today run many of the most dangerous drugs and robbery gangs. She was one of the first illegal arms dealers in the UK to supply high-powered Skorpion machine pistols to her underworld 'clients'.

One source told me that Kel first got hold of the pistols from demobbed British soldiers who fought in Kosovo during the 1990s Balkan conflicts. Some of these weapons had allegedly been stolen by squaddies from the corpses of their enemies. Today, the Skorpion is so well known in the underworld that it has become the must-have weapon for mobsters in the UK.

Kel is now one of the busiest illegal arms suppliers in the UK. But how did she evolve from being a hard-working, tough-talking lady cop into one of this country's most ruthless criminals?

Some serving police officers are convinced that Kel was initially allowed to operate as a criminal by police bosses afraid that she witnessed so much police corruption that she could bring many of them down. One recently retired Kent detective explained: 'A lot of coppers believe Kel was protected by bent coppers who survived the cull which saw her forced into retirement in the first place.'

Kel was dismissed from the police after being caught red-handed supplying a confiscated gun to a well-known British robber in a south London pub. She claimed to her bosses she was trying to nurture the man into becoming an informant, but that didn't wash with her superiors and she was eventually pushed out of The Job.

One of her former colleagues later recalled: 'There was genuine shock when Kel was first nicked. But then her corrupt activities began unravelling. That's when certain senior officers stepped in and pushed her out of the force quietly.'

Some inside the south-east England underworld believe that Kel's past could still come back to haunt her one day. But for the moment, she continues to thrive. 'She's a sassy bird who doesn't take any shit off no one,' said one former Kent bank robber. 'That's why she was a pain in the arse when she was a full-time cozzer. It's not easy trusting someone who was a police officer, especially a bent one. But she's been in this game for a long time now, so she's been accepted by most of us.'

Another one-time professional criminal told me recently: 'Kel once admitted to me that being a gun supplier and a woman is very challenging, but she seems to enjoy it. She said her income has gone up ten-fold since the foreign gangsters turned up in the UK. She doesn't care who her customers are so long as they pay her on time.'

And, it seems, Kel still has some 'old friends' in the south-east's police forces, who are apparently watching her back. As another former detective told me: 'Kel's safe because she knows so much that's never come out. There are a lot of coppers still in The Job who would be implicated in corruption if she decided to tell all.'

Some officers are somewhat surprised that Kel is even still alive. But as one recently retired detective confirmed: 'She's survived because she's never once threatened to tell the full story. That's her trump card.'

However, Kel isn't the only corrupt former police officer with a finger in a lot of crooked pies.

THE SHARK

Many of the most insightful scenes in *Line of Duty* highlight the way that corruption has seeped into every level of the police service. Some serving real-life officers claim this has been grossly exaggerated in the programme for dramatic purposes, but others say it's 'spot on'.

Take 'The Shark'. I can only provide an obscure nickname for him here because there are still a number of allegations swirling around him. Until his retirement a few years back, he was a senior police officer in the south-east of England, which had been at the epicentre of police corruption for many decades.

The Shark had a cluster of high-powered criminals as informants and many current and former police officers remain convinced to this day that he protected those criminals – and even committed and sanctioned crimes on their behalf – in order to keep them on his side.

The Shark's tainted influence has reached right across entire police investigations on multiple occasions. Honest, law-abiding detectives have lost momentum on cases after being forced to release suspects, who'd then cover up any evidence of their involvement in the crimes they were accused of.

It's been alleged that The Shark took a payment of 'at least one hundred thousand pounds' from one notorious criminal informant in exchange for 'burying' murder allegations against a member of that criminal's family. He was also paid huge cash retainers by criminals in order to be their source inside the police force for many years.

As one of his former colleagues later told me: 'The Shark has always believed he was invincible. He used to openly describe some of his activities as simple, old-fashioned policing. He was a master at getting an informant off serious criminal charges if it was of benefit to him in the long run. That man simply has no respect for the word of the law.'

The Shark had the power and influence to get away with it because he held such a senior position inside the force. That meant he could bury evidence against himself and his criminal associates and no one could even challenge his authority. One of his former colleagues explained: 'He told one colleague of mine that he's often broken the law to keep his informants onside. That means he not only threatened people but attacked them as well.'

In *Line of Duty*, ACC Derek Hilton is Ted Hastings' superior officer and overall boss but he eventually turns out to be corrupt himself. 'The Shark makes Hilton in *Line of Duty* look like a schoolboy,' said one of his former colleagues. 'He's a much more impressive character than Hilton, who was greasy and rather cowardly. The Shark exudes confidence and never hesitates over anything.

'He uses his chirpy, talkative character traits to overrun anyone who questions his actions. He's so charming, he makes you feel as if everything he is doing is completely above board.'

Some years back, The Shark was said to have helped cover up a murder allegedly committed by two other corrupt serving police officers. Their target had been an undercover detective, who was on the verge of exposing The Shark and these same two officers. The retired detective explained: 'That murder had The Shark's "prints" all over it. I heard he sanctioned the killing on behalf of himself and his crooked colleagues. They were all clearly prepared to do anything to avoid being exposed as corrupt officers.'

The Shark usually maintains a 'safe' distance from the crimes he's alleged to have committed in order to ensure it is virtually impossible to prove his involvement in such crimes. After all, he is a seasoned detective who knows the importance of not leaving evidence in his wake.

As corruption allegations mounted up against him a few years ago, The Shark was offered a secret early-retirement deal by senior officers. Many of his colleagues were appalled – and remain so to this day. The Shark was effectively permitted to leave the force with an unblemished record and never had to face justice.

'He was so confident they wouldn't expose him that he didn't even want to step down earlier than planned,' explained one former detective colleague. 'So in the end, they gave him a full police pension.'

The Shark very quickly got himself a well-paid job as head of security in the private sector, where he worked for many years on a salary worth five times what he was earning as a police officer. Not surprisingly, he has built up a property empire in the UK and abroad worth at least £10 million. One detective said: 'He's getting on now but seems determined to keep making money. You'd think he'd retire and enjoy all that cash. Maybe he'll keep going until he keels over.'

Even today The Shark – now in his seventies – regularly contacts former police colleagues asking for favours. 'It's incredible,' said one retired detective. 'He comes on the phone as if nothing whatsoever happened and expecting us to drop everything to help. He must in complete denial about what he's done or he simply doesn't give a fuck. It's astounding.'

So, like so many corrupt cops, The Shark seems to be untouchable.

One of his former colleagues spelled it out: 'No doubt he's got a lot of dirt on the top brass and they don't want to upset him in case he turns them over. He's the type of character who'd keep a private file on everyone he's ever worked with. That's his guarantee that he'll never be exposed.'

Until there's a knock at the door…

DONALD URQUART

Contract killings are a recurring and disturbing fact of life when it comes to real-life *Line of Duty*-style police corruption. But one of the most chilling executions in London underworld history marked a disturbing 'sea change' when it came to bent cops.

It was 1993 and corrupt officers were alleged to be involved in a vast array of crimes, as well as being on the payroll of some of the most ruthless professional criminals this country has ever seen.

'Businessman' Donald Urquhart had connections to a vast money-laundering ring after working with professional robbers who pulled off some of the most spectacular heists of the 1980s. He also had some wealthy 'associates' in Colombia.

Urquhart was a former hod carrier who claimed to have built up his fortune thanks to the property boom of the 1970s and 1980s. He'd also become a middleman between corrupt officers and crime bosses.

Scotland Yard investigators knew Urquhart had other

'interests' through his numerous bank accounts in the Cayman Islands and Jersey tax havens. Some of those accounts had been used to facilitate corrupt police officers with illicit payments. At least two high-ranking Scotland Yard officers had offshore bank accounts set up for them by Urquhart because they were being paid such large amounts of money.

One former London detective explained: 'This guy Urquhart knew everything there was to know about bent cops. He had all the paperwork and he was the man who met them, passed over envelopes of cash.' In the autumn of 1992, Donald Urquhart was warned by corrupt police officers that his life might be in danger because one of their cocaine-addicted crooked 'colleagues' had become so paranoid that he was convinced Urquhart was about to inform on him to senior police investigators.

'He was correct, of course,' one former London detective later told me. 'Urquhart was about to become a full-time police informant. He'd decided to grass everyone up because he was so scared he was about to be killed.'

In November 1992, Urquhart was warned by London police officers that a team of criminals and corrupt police officers were shadowing him. The same detective explained: 'But he refused to be put under protection immediately because he had some dodgy stuff he wanted to get done first.'

Then just after Christmas of the same year, Urquhart told police it was time to hand himself in. That's when the countdown to the end of his life began. 'Urquhart was playing everyone off against each other. Now he wanted us to protect him and he wanted immunity from prosecution.

That sort of deal doesn't happen overnight,' explained another former detective.

A few days later, Urquhart and his girlfriend left their local pub in Marylebone, central London, after a drink together. Two men on a scooter passed them on the cobblestones of a deserted, dimly lit mews. One pulled out a gun as the bike slowed down.

Urquhart was shot three times and died at the scene as his hysterical girlfriend tried to revive him.

When detectives examined Urquhart's car parked outside his home, they found it contained three telephones and a fax machine. He'd turned the vehicle into a mobile office for his so-called business deals because he was so worried about his own personal security.

The motivation and method used to kill Urquhart, fifty-five, on the streets of west London was in itself an alarm call for London's police. Being gunned down by a man riding pillion on a scooter was a classic South American method. But that turned out to be a deliberate move by the London criminals and corrupt officers on Urquhart's tail, who wanted it to look like the Colombians had a score to settle.

It later transpired that the gun used in the killing was most likely supplied by a corrupt policeman-turned-underworld-gun-dealer who shall have to remain nameless. But it was not until some years later that detectives were told by one well-known criminal that corrupt officers had encouraged the hit on Urquhart because they feared he was about to expose them.

'These crooked cops wound up their crime boss paymasters

into believing that Urquhart – who handled a lot of the cartel cash in Europe – was about to inform police about their drug empire,' explained one London detective. 'Sure, Urquhart was a professional criminal working for some dangerous characters, but that doesn't mean he deserved to die in cold blood.'

Later, it emerged that Urquhart had wanted to tell police everything because he believed one particular corrupt detective was planning to have him killed rather than risk exposure.

One corrupt cop told me one time: 'You know you're committing a truly cardinal sin but you can't help yourself when you go bent. That fear and terror then drives you to commit awful crimes in desperation.'

No one has ever been convicted for the murder of Donald Urquhart.

SPIDER

Drugs are undoubtedly the root of all evil when it comes to police corruption. Former-detective-turned-narco Spider is a classic example of the damage they can do.

I can't even reveal which force Spider served with or his rank because it would give away his identity. Since leaving the police in the 1990s, he has served time in prison in Spain for providing 'help' to some of Britain's most powerful cocaine barons.

Tracking down corrupt officers with connections to the deadly world of cocaine is harder than getting to the actual gangsters themselves. Most are extremely reluctant to break cover because they would then be in mortal danger from their own crooked and straight colleagues, as well as the criminals they work for. Spider only agreed to talk to me because a number of his associates had vouched for me.

Our first meeting took place in a quiet pub close to Spider's home in south-east England. Spider said he'd initially (and not surprisingly) endured some very tricky moments in prison after being targeted by other inmates for being a 'bent copper'. But he managed to win round even the most ruthless of criminals eventually by agreeing to provide common sense 'advice' to incarcerated criminals on how to successfully deal in drugs on their release from prison. 'Doing that guaranteed me around-the-clock protection,' explained Spider. 'I had to get them on my side, so I was prepared to do just about anything, otherwise they would have made my life hell.'

But it was Spider's corrupt dealings with some of the UK's most powerful cocaine barons that interested me the most.

'How did these criminals turn you corrupt in the first place?' I asked him.

'Oh, it's all very predictable, really,' answered Spider. 'I was dealing with those type of villains virtually every day as a detective in a drugs squad, but I carefully avoided taking any bribes for a long time. I really believed I could stay straight.'

Spider arrested a couple of criminals who were part of a big cocaine smuggling gang and one of them mentioned that his boss would pay big money for some information.

He went on: 'I just laughed it off at first because I'd heard about guys like this offering bribes to cops many times before.

I couldn't actually believe they'd be stupid enough to try it on me, though.'

But Spider had recently developed a serious secret cocaine habit after busting a number of high-profile drugs gangs. He explained: 'I'd gone undercover and that involved having to snort coke in order to be accepted into a circle of criminals. Trouble is, I liked the stuff too much! It made me feel confident and positive and, quite frankly, for a while I actually think it improved my skills as a detective!

'Cocaine addiction creeps up on you when you least expect it to. You believe you can control it, but it ends up controlling you. You go home at night thinking you won't take any more until you're out partying with yer mates, but then you get tempted to take a line to get through the day and that's when it takes you over.'

Soon, cocaine was impacting on every aspect of Spider's life, even though he didn't realise it at the time. 'I was in complete denial about the damage I was doing to myself. And that's when I got even more "vulnerable", as they call it in the force.'

Spider's modest police salary simply didn't pay enough to cover his drug habit and support his wife and two young children.

'It was causing no end of problems at home,' he explained. 'Obviously my wife didn't know I was hooked on coke. She thought I was having an affair with someone at work and the atmosphere at home was toxic. Our two small children had no idea what was going on. But I was either high as a kite or in a bad temper from coke-comedown, so I wasn't exactly being a loving father, either.'

Desperate to feed his coke habit and equally desperate to feed his wife and family, Spider contacted a professional criminal who'd once offered him 'good money' if he could help him with 'a few favours' after they met when police raided that same gangster's property in the Home Counties.

Spider recalled: 'This guy was a big player in the cocaine trade and he liked to keep one step ahead of his friends and enemies. I knew exactly what I was getting myself into and I was desperate to keep my family together and continue taking coke. I felt I had no choice, even though it was all my fault in the first place.'

A meeting in the car park of a motorway service station followed. Spider recalled: 'This villain had an appalling record for violence, including an attack on a policeman. But I was so deep in a hole by this time that I didn't really care. I just wanted money and I would do pretty much anything to get it.'

Within weeks, Spider had been 'pulled in hook, line and sinker' by his underworld paymaster. He told me: 'It was easy money at first. I'd trace a few car registrations then swap that info for an envelope with £500 in it. I actually convinced myself it wasn't harming anyone particularly. What an idiot I was!

Not surprisingly, the information demanded by Spider's gangster paymaster soon became much more sensitive. 'He wanted to know things like details of a statement given against him by another criminal. It was obvious he was going to do something to that other gangster, who was going to give evidence against him.

'I was endangering a man's life just for a few bob. Now I look back on what I did with disgust at myself. How could I have been such a cold bastard? But my cocaine addiction was driving me on all the time. I had to have at least two grams on me at all times. It made me feel invincible, as if I was in complete control of my own destiny. How stupid is that?'

He heard allegations that his gangster paymaster regularly used firearms to 'threaten and harm' his underworld enemies. Spider recalled: 'This guy was charming to me, but in a very cold way. But I just ignored it. Looking back on it, he was one of the most dangerous criminals I'd ever met. I even knew my own life would be in danger if I ever crossed him. But I still didn't seem to care.'

Then Spider's crime boss told him he was so impressed with the illicit information being provided that he was recommending Spider's 'services' to other gangsters in the south-east. 'I should have backed away there and then but I wanted the money, so I played along with him,' said Spider.

Soon, other gangsters were using Spider for his 'services' and they were often paying him in thousands rather than hundreds. But it was often for much more sensitive, inside information.

By this time Spider's consumption of coke had 'gone up tenfold'. He explained: 'I'd turned into a physical wreck, barely able to operate on a day-to-day basis. I was only sleeping a couple of hours each night because I was so high on cocaine. I was a complete mess.'

Spider believes the cocaine killed his ability to under-stand the consequences of his actions. 'I went into a state of cocaine-induced denial, I guess. I tried my hardest not to think about how the confidential police information I was providing to those criminals was being used. I should have called a halt there and then but I needed more and more cash to take as much coke as I could and still provide for my family. But I knew inside myself that it couldn't go on for ever.'

He went on: 'I'd become the copper these criminals could actually trust and they were virtually queuing up to use my services.'

And there was one very advantageous spin-off from Spider's corrupt activities: 'These same criminals tipped me off about rival criminals who they wanted removed from the streets. I actually had a higher arrest record at that stage than virtually all my colleagues and it was mainly down to being a bent copper.'

For the following two years, Spider earned more than £200,000 in bribes from cocaine gangs. He explained: 'I should have recognised that the things I was being asked to do would eventually lead back to me, but I just kept going without ever stopping to think about such issues.'

By this time, Spider was using the UK police computer to access bank accounts, phone records, police reports on known criminals. He was even able to access witness statements in big drug cases. 'It was crazy and very dangerous,' he said. 'Many people could be harmed when this information leaked into the hands of professional criminals.'

Then one of the UK's most notorious drug barons began using Spider's 'services'. He explained: 'I got a very big payment from this one gangster when I got him some information on one of his biggest underworld enemies.'

But that information supplied by Spider led directly to a shooting. No one was actually killed but the incident sparked a very thorough police investigation and that's when his activities were finally flagged up.

Spider recalled: 'Looking back at it, I probably would have died of cocaine poisoning if I hadn't been busted. I was taking as much as ten grams a day while juggling my work as a detective with a young family, all of whom were sick of me coming home late at night drunk and coked out of my mind.'

Then two detectives turned up at Spider's family home and told him they knew all about his corrupt activities.

'I was so relieved,' he explained. 'I'd had enough of hiding everything from the people I love and from my colleagues. I needed help but up until that point I'd been too scared to ask.'

Spider was then booked into a drug clinic to get him off cocaine and alcohol while detectives began investigating all his criminal activities and connections. He recalled: 'I'd been so off my head on coke most of the time, I'd barely noticed what I was up to. I didn't even keep count of how many times I'd taken a bribe.'

Spider was told he would face multiple criminal charges but any jail sentence could be greatly reduced if he co-operated with the investigation. His situation was a closely guarded secret because of fears that his onetime criminal clients might decide to kill him to prevent him informing the police about their activities.

'My biggest priority was to protect my family,' he explained. 'They didn't deserve any of this. They had no idea what I'd been up to. I did a deal with the investigating officers but I knew there were a lot of issues involved, which were completely out of my control.'

But first he had to admit everything to his wife. 'I was very lucky she stuck by me. I didn't deserve it. I'd let everyone down. I can't really ever forgive myself for doing that.'

Meanwhile, Spider's gangster 'customers' continued to pose a real threat to his safety and that of his family. He explained: 'Those criminals were worried I was going to name them, so I had to make a really hard decision: I backed out of doing a deal with the police. I could have spilled the beans and got a lighter sentence or I could protect my family's safety and just accept a longer sentence, which was inevitable for failing to fully co-operate with my colleagues.'

Even some of Spider's betrayed former colleagues genuinely sympathised with his dilemma. He explained: 'They all knew that my life and that of my family was in danger if I provided the names of those criminals who'd bribed me. I didn't want to protect them but I felt I had no choice.'

When Spider was handed down a 'lengthy sentence' he took it philosophically: 'I knew they had to make an example of me. I hope that what happened to me will put off any other young coppers tempted to accept a bribe, then at least something good has come out of all this. My main priority was to serve my sentence and then get out and be with my family once again. I got what I deserved. I have no complaints about the way I was treated by the police. I had broken the golden rule in every sense of the word.

'But the way I look at it is that I'm lucky to be alive. If I hadn't been busted as a bent copper, I could well have ended up dying from a cocaine overdose and then where would my family have been?'

'I've met many professional criminals. I have dealt with them first-hand and I can tell you that none of the big players would hesitate to kill if someone got in their way. The only reason I survived is because I didn't squeal on them.'

Today, Spider lives a quiet, reserved life in Middle England. His children are now grown up. He works occasionally as a gardener and his wife has a full-time job. 'She's stuck by me through thick and thin and proved beyond doubt that there is nothing more important in your life than your family.'

But the UK's richest gangsters and their corrupt police associates thrive on a much higher level of finance and danger than the Spiders of this world.

ANT THE CLEANER

Line of Duty is located in a gritty undisclosed northern-type city, so injecting billionaire criminals into the show's plot lines might not seem particularly relevant.

But these mega-weathy gangsters help to feed entire criminal enterprises. Take money launderer Ant. He's a West Country born and bred ex-drug baron who now operates one of the UK's biggest cash-cleaning operations.

Ant has corrupt police officers on his books because they're a vital part of his empire. He explained: 'Crooked cops are needed by myself and my very rich clientele because they can often get things done below the radar, so to speak.

Sometimes I need to get my clients out of sticky situations with the police, so a corrupt officer prepared to lose some evidence for a cash bribe is worth more than his weight in gold.'

Ant also pays corrupt police officers for covert information about his own 'business rivals' as well as carrying out unofficial due diligence checks on any potential new clients who want him to launder their cash. 'Some of these corrupt officers come to me through private investigators, but I prefer to deal direct with them because the less people involved the better as that means less chance of exposure.'

Ant sometimes deals with tens of millions of pounds in cash during one single transaction. And he doesn't deny that a lot of his clients' money comes from the proceeds of crime.

He claims there is even an unofficial 'database' of corrupt police officers in the south-east of England who are available for work in exchange for bribes. 'Obviously, it's not something people talk about openly but it can be assessed with special link codes. But I don't hire corrupt cops through it myself because I'm suspicious that it may have been set up by the police themselves to try and trap crooked officers.'

But while money laundering may not sound on the surface as dangerous as the drugs game, there have been many unexplained deaths in the UK connected to it in recent years, including one of Ant's closest associates.

He explained: 'This guy was one of my middlemen who dealt on a day-to-day basis with half a dozen oligarchs, who live mainly in London, as well as a number of Chinese billionaires.' These 'clients' were paying between 10 and 20 per cent of all their cash in commission to Ant and his team of launderers. That could often mean he earned millions of pounds a month in fees.

Ant continued: 'But we had to be super-careful. There was one particular oligarch whom we knew was being watched by the UK police and security services. He had close ties to a very powerful Russian politician.'

One of Ant's corrupt police officers even warned him that this particular oligarch might get them into trouble, so they tried to pull away from him. 'But this oligarch got very upset with my middleman because – as far as he was concerned – we were locked into him for life. He was also deeply paranoid that we knew too much about him.'

Then one day the Oligarch summoned Ant's middleman and started making threats against him and Ant. 'I went back to my corrupt cop and asked him for advice,' Ant explained. 'He agreed to try and access police computer records on this man. We found references to his activities via a surveillance report. He was mixed up with some very heavy characters.

'So now we knew we were in dangerous waters. Also, my corrupt cop warned me that the UK police and security services might shut us down as well because of our contact with that oligarch.'

So Ant approached one of the highest-ranking corrupt police officers in the UK for help.

Ant recalled: 'He was so high up, we could only talk to him via three middlemen. I explained to him that we needed to get this oligarch thrown out of Britain before he tried to kill either me or my middleman or both of us.'

But Ant's crooked senior cop demanded to be paid 'a shit load of cash first'. He also demanded that Ant supplied confidential information about the oligarch as leverage against him if there was any comeback.

Ant explained: 'My back was against the wall so I mistakenly handed over some very confidential stuff to the crooked cop. His bosses immediately broke their promises of confidentiality and used the information I'd provided to put pressure on the oligarch. He knew immediately that the leak must have come from my organisation.'

Ant hoped the oligarch would be thrown out of the UK before he had time to launch a revenge attack.

'But nothing happened to him and he remained in London,' he explained. 'It was only later I discovered that the oligarch was paying other corrupt UK cops and security officials to guarantee that he could stay in the UK in exchange for information he would tell them about that Russian politician. He even had a corrupt official inside the Home Office.

'Myself and my middleman went into a complete lockdown. We had six bodyguards with us at all times of the day and night because my own corrupt cop warned me that it was now likely the oligarch would come after us.'

But Ant's middleman had a cocaine and gambling problem, which made him much more 'vulnerable' than Ant. Eventually, he forced the middleman to move into an isolated house in the country so he could go 'cold turkey' to cure his drug addiction.

'But he was soon sneaking into London to buy drugs and gamble,' explained Ant. 'In the end, I had to pull all the security off him to teach him a lesson. It was a gamble but I had to do something to stop him behaving so irresponsibly. He didn't take much notice, though.'

Ant went on: 'One night, he came home to the house in the country with a bag of coke and two hookers. Within minutes, he was out cold. Then the two women let a number of men into the house. He woke up to find himself being dangled over the edge of a bedroom balcony by the men. They must have wanted to know what the police and UK security services had been told about the oligarch and his activities.

'I have no idea if he told them anything but he didn't know much, so I'd guess they got a bit frustrated with his answers. They then pulled him back onto the balcony, pointed a gun to his head and gave him a choice: either jump or get a bullet in the head.

'He jumped and ended up impaled on the railings, fifty foot below. He didn't stand a chance. The oligarch himself sent me a condolence note and referred to my partner's death as a tragic "Russian Suicide".

'Apparently it's the Russian underworld's favourite method of murdering someone because if people think you committed suicide, it's more shaming for the family.'

Yet despite all this, Ant continued washing money for many associates of the same oligarch after he left the UK. 'I have to be realistic. These billionaires clearly had a hold over the London police and security services which had helped many of them to be untouchable.

'One corrupt cop told that before the oligarch finally left, he'd been double dealing with UK police and security services about the movements of his political friends in Moscow. This apparently gave him a Get Out of Jail card, even though he was most likely behind the murder of my friend.'

Ant recently quit all contact with his corrupt police officers and secretly 'sold' his business to an up-and-coming younger drug baron with aspirations to become a money launderer on a vast scale.

'I shaped the deal so it doesn't even look as though I have left the laundering operation,' Ant explained. 'It was the only way I could get out without my clients coming after me.'

But there are many others connected to police corruption who end up paying the inevitable price.

LEM

In *Line of Duty*, corrupt police are shown as being capable of anything, even murder, but it usually all happens within a police environment.

We've already explored that the worst can often happen after they've left the force, and this was certainly the case for cardinal sinner Lem.

Within just a few years of 'retiring' from the police, Lem had a collection of seven cars, including a Ferrari and a Bentley, parked in the driveway of his detached home near Birmingham. He described himself as a 'property developer'. His nickname 'Lem' referred to the yellowy colour of his skin, which was rumoured to be the result of too many visits to his local tanning salon.

And Lem constantly boasted about the number of former

police colleagues he had on his payroll. But then he needed all the protection he could get.

His family had been victims of a kidnap attempt by London gangsters after he fell out with them over a 'business deal'. One criminal I know in the Midlands told me that the London mobsters had been encouraged to target Lem and his family by two corrupt London police officers, who claimed they were owed more than £100,000 by Lem.

No wonder other criminals in the Midlands labelled Lem 'a fuckin' liability'.

Back in 2007, Lem's latest property scam required some much-needed financial backing, so he visited a few well-known faces in the Midlands, including a couple of retired UK police detectives. He was hoping to persuade them to invest in a timeshare resort he planned to build in Montenegro.

Lem waxed lyrical to all his old criminal associates in the Midlands about the opportunities in Eastern Europe by comparing Montenegro to Spain twenty or thirty years earlier. 'Cheap land and cheap labour and you can do anything you want if you bung the right people,' he told them all.

Lem's potential business partners – including those two retired detectives – even hired a corrupt London-cop-turned-private-investigator to do some 'due diligence' checks on Lem and his Montenegro property scheme.

It then transpired that he had not only ripped off other business partners in the past, but he also had a penchant for violence. One former business partner was rumoured to have been crippled for life after a 'disagreement' with Lem following the sale of a detached house near Lem's hometown of Coventry.

The corrupt officer who was checking out Lem also came across an allegation that Lem was an informant for the US's much-feared Drug Enforcement Administration, whose agents had for decades been spying on the drug trade in the UK and Europe.

It was becoming clear that Lem was playing a dangerous game. He was then spotted having lunch with two former police colleagues, who were well known in the UK underworld for providing 'safe' transportation for drug shipments.

Not surprisingly, Lem's potential business partners then all decided they didn't want to invest in his Montenegro timeshare development. Lem insisted he didn't care. He claimed he had plenty of other investors lined up and was going out to Montenegro anyway to finalise the timeshare property deal within the next few days.

In April 2007, Lem and an associate travelled to Montenegro with two of their supposed investors, who wanted to view the secluded site where the proposed timeshare development was going to be built. All four men boarded a specially hired twin-engine Cessna 310 at Biggin Hill Airport, in Kent.

The Cessna aircraft lost contact with air-traffic controllers minutes before it was due to land at the coastal city of Tivat. Within hours, the Montenegro air force and police began searching a 200 km-square area for the missing aircraft but there was no sign of Lem, his associates or the plane. None were ever found.

One of the criminals who'd been approached by Lem to invest in his timeshare business told me a few years later:

'Lem was a liability. Many of us thought he was setting us up to be nicked by the DEA, so someone took the appropriate action. End of story.'

SPUD

It's clear from the carefully structured plotlines that run throughout the five series of *Line of Duty* that most corrupt cops ultimately find themselves trapped in a vicious circle. In real-life police corruption, too, there are many self-destructive characters who make themselves vulnerable to extortion, which ultimately often leads to police corruption.

Spud is a classic example. He was working long hours, shelling out for a huge mortgage, and had a reputation for being a 'prime thief-taker.' But gradually he was being sucked into a familiar shady world of drugs, gambling and prostitutes.

Spud explained: 'Like so many coppers, I'd discovered cocaine after going undercover inside a drugs gang. I had no choice but to take the coke that was offered to me, otherwise I would have been sussed out.

'The beauty of cocaine is that you can function on it and appear reasonably normal, so your colleagues don't usually have a clue what you're up to. In many ways, it would have been better if I'd got hooked on heroin, then at least my colleagues would have found out much sooner that I had a drug problem and maybe I could have sorted it all out.

'But coke became the fuel which drove me on to achieve bigger and better things in my job. I didn't even consider that buying coke off a dealer was totally out of order, especially for a copper. I needed the coke to operate at full strength, so I just didn't care.'

Gradually, Spud began staying out late at night when he was supposed to be at home with his family. 'My life revolved around nicking villains and taking coke, although not necessarily in that order. In order to get easy access to cocaine I became a regular at some really sleazy nightclubs. I even convinced myself that I was more likely to bring the bad guys to justice if I nurtured people involved in the world of drugs and hookers. I thought I could control the coke and booze, but it was taking over my life.'

Then the inevitable happened.

Spud explained: 'I ended up in a notorious west London brothel with two hookers and a bag of coke. How predictable was that? I was so off my head, I'd even snorted coke off their bodies and I'd been open about being a cop and having a laugh about it with the barman and then the two girls I slept with.

'When I left the brothel off my face, two men approached me as I got into my car and said they'd recorded and filmed every moment of my encounter with the women. I was so high, I told them to fuck off. Next morning, I woke up wondering if it had really happened at all and then struggled into work with a head-splitting hangover.'

Spud continued: 'I was on my third cup of coffee and my colleagues were taking the piss because I looked so wrecked, when my boss pulled me into his office. He said an envelope had been delivered to him containing photos of me walking in and out of the brothel. They didn't show any dirty stuff but I knew this was a warning.'

At first Spud tried to claim he'd been following a suspect, but his boss knew he was lying because he hadn't even been on duty the previous night.

He recalled: 'I was embarrassed and ashamed that my boss now knew all about my dirty habits. But he was very good about it. We talked man to man and he said he wouldn't tell anyone and that we should carry on as if nothing had happened.

'I was surprised by his attitude because he'd always seemed very straight, but I was extremely grateful.'

But – despite this close shave – Spud still couldn't put a lid on his drug habit. 'I was back in the office bathroom a few minutes after talking to my boss and snorted virtually half a gram in one line. Coke was becoming like a tranquilliser for me in a sense. It helped drown out all the problems in my head.'

A few days later, Spud's boss asked him out for a pint at a local pub. Spud recalled: 'I was surprised because we'd never socialised before. Anyway, we sat down in a quiet corner of the pub and then he slipped a sachet of coke under the table to me. I was astonished.

'At first I thought it was his version of tough love or that he was trying to trap me in some way. But I couldn't have been more wrong.'

Then came the bombshell. Spud's boss's face went stony as he informed Spud there was more coke where that came from. All he had to do was 'cause a few problems' for another detective, whom he said was on the take.

Spud went on: 'I was stunned. Sure I'd become a cokehead with a drink problem but I'd never once considered doing anything dodgy like that. It appalled me.'

Spud's boss noticed the look on his face and then went in for the kill.

'He told me, "I've got all the tapes and footage of you inside that knocking shop, son. You need to get real here. All you've gotta do is make sure that bloke gets what he deserves for being bent." After he'd said that, I knew I was completely fucked. I had nowhere to turn, so I agreed to help him frame that officer.'

It was only later he discovered that his boss was in fact the corrupt cop, not his colleague who had been threatening to expose Spud's boss. 'I was stunned. My boss had been stringing me along and he was bent all along. I'd been roped in and there was no turning back. I needed the money, so I played the game.'

Over the following two years, Spud became the 'go-to man' for criminals wanting sensitive information from the police computer. Meanwhile at home things were going from bad to worse. 'My wife demanded a divorce. My kids wouldn't speak to me and my boss – the man who'd fucked my life up in the first place – just kept reminding me that I had to help him and other corrupt officers and criminals.'

Spud's corrupt activities only finally came to light when he was involved in a car crash while driving over the limit on drink and drugs. 'I was quite badly injured and ended up in ICU. That was my wake-up call,' he explained. 'I guess in some ways, it was a cry for help.'

Anti-corruption unit officers soon visited Spud in hospital. He refused to co-operate at first. 'I was terrified that those bent coppers including my boss might kill me if I spoke out.'

Then Spud's corrupt boss went round to see his wife at the family home and told her he was worried about her husband's health. Spud explained: 'She was very upset. His visit to our home freaked me out. I realised it was a message from him that he and his crooked cop mates and their criminal friends would get to my family if I spoke out about corruption.'

For the following few days, Spud lay in that hospital bed, petrified. Then early one morning, a nurse discovered him in a hospital toilet, trying to open the window.

He explained: 'She knew immediately that I was planning to jump and gently and very kindly talked me out of doing it. I have no doubt that those corrupt cops would have loved it if I'd jumped.'

Spud was understandably distraught. He knew he had to somehow wipe the slate clean if he was to stand any chance of surviving.

He described what he did next: 'That night, I contacted the anti-corruption guys and told them I was willing to help them on one condition – myself and my family would need protection.'

Within three days, Spud was out of hospital and he and his family were living in a safe house while new identities were organised. He went on: 'When I left the hospital, I thanked the nurse who stopped me committing suicide. She said she hoped the criminals who were after me would be brought to justice.

'"Criminals?" I replied. '"They're police officers."

'I've never forgotten the look of horror on her face. Out

there in the real world people expect the police to be honest and upstanding. It was such a shock to her.'

At the safe house, anti-corruption officers showed Spud chilling video surveillance footage of his crooked police boss arriving at the family house and discovering that it was empty and his family had all gone. 'You could hear him shouting and swearing as he walked back to his car,' Spud said. 'He must have known then that I'd decided to give evidence against him and other corrupt officers.'

In the underworld, it was rumoured that a price had been put on the heads of Spud and his family. They were assigned armed police guards to protect them around the clock.

Spud recalled: 'A few days later, my corrupt boss disappeared before he'd even been interviewed. No one knows what happened to him. The anti-corruption unit believed he'd either been kidnapped by his criminal associates or committed suicide.'

Once Spud's boss was off the scene, he felt more secure and eventually his evidence helped bring down a gang of criminals, but allegedly the corrupt officers were not prosecuted because of 'lack of evidence'.

He continued: 'But there was a very high price to pay for all this. My children never forgave me for the way I behaved during my "cocaine years". My wife has stuck by me but admits she can't trust me ever again. I've tried all sorts of new jobs from taxi driving to carpentry but none of them match the excitement and importance of being a police officer.

'And even today, I'm never fully relaxed because I know there are people out there who'd like to harm me and my family and the realisation that it is entirely my fault is very hard to deal with.'

In recent years, he has become an ardent fan of TV's *Line of Duty*. He said: 'I like the show a lot. Many of my former colleagues think it is a bit over the top but I know from first-hand experience that police corruption makes people do really terrible things.

'My only criticism of the show is that it doesn't really contain much about the victims of police corruption like the families of bent cops and their victims.'

Back in the real world, there are some corrupt police officers who try to let their law-abiding colleagues do all their dirty work for them.

MICHAEL BOYLE

In the 1990s, *Line of Duty*'s Ted Hastings' Northern Ireland homeland was inhabited by some real-life terrorists, whose influence would eventually reach across the sea and into the London underworld. One of these criminals was at the centre of a chilling example of corruption that rocked the capital's police force.

By the mid-1990s, many of the terrorists who inhabited the streets of Northern Ireland's cities were running out of work, thanks to the ongoing peace process. Some of them offered themselves as marksmen-for-hire to old-school professional gangs of criminals on the mainland.

That's how one freelance killer from 'across the water' found himself in the middle of a doomed police surveillance operation in east London that would expose a stunning myriad of corrupt police activity that seems unbelievable, except it all really happened.

It began in August 1994 when two totally innocent London citizens called Peter McCormack and John Ogden were shot dead in Cavendish Road, Balham, in the south-west of the city. The police believed they were killed by mistake because one of them bore a striking resemblance to a south London criminal, whose problems with a local crime family had led to a number of earlier unsolved gangland killings.

A few months after the McCormack and Ogden murders, Irish National Liberation Army terrorist Michael Boyle – an armed kidnapper and known killer with lengthy prison terms behind him in Ireland – was hired for £25,000 from across the water to murder the head of that same crime family. Boyle had also worked as an intelligence gatherer for the Provisional IRA. In prison in Ireland, he'd rubbed shoulders with some of the most dangerous terrorists in the world.

One detective who was close to the case later told me that Boyle had been commissioned after two corrupt police officers put pressure on their criminal associates. They wanted the south London crime boss murdered because he was threatening to expose their corrupt practices to their police bosses.

As one recently retired south London detective explained: 'These bent coppers were shitting it and thought they were about to get turned over. As a result, they were prepared to do anything to get that local gangster off the streets because he was mouthing it off that he was going to finish them off.'

These corrupt officers knew from colleagues that the same south London gangster was actually being tailed by law-abiding police at that time. 'But they didn't actually care,' explained one former south London detective. 'They wanted this guy dead, whatever it took.'

A few days later, the legitimate police surveillance team watched as the target walked out of his family home in Rotherhithe, south-east London. Just then, Irish hitman Michael Boyle stepped out from behind a bush and began pumping bullets into him.

'The detectives shadowing that gangster were stunned,' explained one former detective. 'They immediately drew their own weapons and forcibly stopped Boyle's shooting spree.'

Boyle was hit by five shots but he and his intended victim both survived.

It later emerged that those corrupt officers had wrongly presumed that the honest detectives tailing that same gangster would simply step back and enable Boyle to do his job.

As the retired south London detective explained: 'They hadn't even thought about the danger to their colleagues if Boyle had shot at those officers. Bent coppers often can't see the light for the day because they are so immersed in duplicity. They actually believed the police unit following that gangster would allow him to be killed because he was such a hated figure.'

As one well-known south-east London face later said: 'That gangster was a lucky boy to have the police watching his back, literally. We was all amazed that he survived and it was all down to those cozzers. But then we heard rumours about those bent cops being involved in commissioning Boyle in the first place.'

Following his arrest, Boyle called a detective to his cell at Belmarsh high-security prison in south-east London and revealed the names of his alleged paymasters. He claimed he'd been hired directly by an Irish gangster who told him that his target was 'treading on a lot of toes' while expanding his drugs cartel in south-east London.

Then police discovered the same gangster target had been threatening to expose the same two corrupt London cops behind the hit. They'd in fact approached an Irish gangster to hire Boyle for the job, so there was sufficient 'distance' between themselves and the would-be shooter.

Michael Boyle was eventually jailed for life at the Old Bailey for attempting to murder that London gangster. He was ordered to serve a minimum of fifteen years. However, rumours that the hit had been set up by renegade detectives continued to dog the case, even when I was working on a book about the south London underworld some years later.

As one detective who served at that time told me: 'That hitman case sums up how deep police corruption went back in the mid-1990s. It was an extraordinary state of affairs but certain detectives back then would have gone to any lengths to hide their corrupt practices.'

And there's one stretch of sunny coastline, which has become the ultimate hiding place for corrupt cops and many of their criminal associates.

COSTA DEL CRIME

Line of Duty hasn't so far filmed at any locations outside the UK. But if and when the writers decide to expand the show's location base you can be sure that Spain's notorious southern coastline – long known as the Costa del Crime – will be one of their first ports of call.

I've spent much of the past twenty-five years driving up and down the coastline of this so-called sunshine paradise, meeting an assortment of criminals and retired police officers, many of whom live just a few miles from each other.

I discovered long ago that interviewing such characters away from the UK can lead to much more frank and open discussions, especially over a beer in a sparkling yacht marina or a shady hillside taverna.

One old-school ex-bank robber who lives in the mountains behind Marbella put it this way: 'You let yer guard down more in a place like this. The rainy old London underworld seems a million miles away, so you're often more open about what you're up to.'

Many of the big names in the robbery and kidnap 'game' of the 1970s and 80s moved here with their ill-gotten gains. They say this sunny slice of the Mediterranean can be fraught with danger in many ways. The same ex-bank robber explained: 'Down here, you walk into a bar and find yourself sitting opposite some bastard bent copper who nicked you thirty or forty years ago and you have to swallow it.

'Often the problem is that anything goes in a place like this. The Spanish police don't give a toss about what you get up to as long as you make sure they get the occasional "drink".'

Many criminals I've spoken to on the so-called Costa del Crime reckon that Spanish police officers are even more corrupt than their British counterparts, thanks to extremely low salaries and a more lenient attitude towards drugs. One Marbella police detective I interviewed a few years back insisted I paid him a bribe otherwise he wouldn't help me with my enquiries into the murder of a British criminal.

And when one British crime boss went on the run in Spain in 1996, he was helped by corrupt detectives from both countries. It was later alleged this same crime boss had regularly paid bribes to these officers for many years. During the hunt for him, police in both Spain and the UK even shut down all their normal lines of communications because they feared this crime boss's 'friends' in the police of both countries might let him know if police were on his tail.

One retired bank 'blagger' told me a few years back that some professional robbers went broke because they had to spend most of their proceeds on paying off corrupt police officers. A lot of those bent cops ended up retiring to Spain.

'The bent ex-British cops I've come across down here in Spain are often the types who'll shoot you without thinking twice if they suspect you're gonna try and turn them over,' one Marbella-based bank robber explained.

One Madrid-based judge who specialises in targeting the European underworld told me recently that he tried to have four crooked former British police officers arrested after they were detained for acting suspiciously while working 'in a private security capacity' in southern Spain. They were eventually expelled because Spanish authorities believed they were about to commit 'a very significant crime'.

But when it comes to corrupt UK police officers living on the Costa del Crime, there is one who really stands out in the crowd.

GRINDER

In October 2019, a former cop, known as 'The Grinder' for good reason, emailed me when he heard I was working on the Costa del Sol and invited me for dinner at his house for a catch-up.

I'd been talking to Grinder for more than twenty-five years, during which he provided a lot of vital information for my numerous true crime books. This is a character who makes corrupt officer John Corbett – played with such force by Stephen Graham in series five of *Line of Duty* – look relatively harmless.

Grinder has always claimed he's NOT corrupt but was labelled as such by duplicitous colleagues after he infiltrated a gang of renegade crooked officers to help his bosses bring them to justice.

They claimed he *was* the corrupt officer, not them. However, most of them were eventually given early retirement rather than being arrested, so it's impossible to know who was really telling the truth.

When I visited Grinder at his detached villa in 2019, I could immediately see that he'd made a lot more money than most police officers. His detached villa was surrounded by high walls and had a speakerphone on the pillar next to the wrought-iron electronically operated front gates. Inside the grounds was a substantial property complete with swimming pool, long driveway and a tennis court. There were even scanning CCTVs dotted around every few yards, plus two Rottweilers who bounded out of the back door of the villa when I drew up in my rental car.

Grinder – in his seventies – looked no different from the first day I met him more than a quarter of a century earlier. Even the receding hairline was the same.

So I settled on a sun-lounger by the side of his pool and we began talking about the good old days when dodgy police detectives like himself could literally get away with murder.

'I don't deny I had to pull a few stunts back then but I wasn't a bent copper like they all tried to make out,' he explained, as he chopped up some cucumber and tomatoes next to his beloved barbeque. 'But the "rules" of the game were very different back then,' he said. 'You had to do certain things in order to put the bad guys away.'

That was always Grinder's excuse. Like so many old-school police detectives from 'back in the day' he defended his 'dodgy' work practices by claiming there was no other way to bring villains to justice.

'I've heard it said that I helped arrange a hitman to knock off some villain who was upsetting one of my informants,' said Grinder, sipping from a bottle of San Miguel. 'That is total crap. Sure, I turned the other cheek when my informants got up to some mischief but would I really be stupid enough to book a hitman for a job? I don't think so.'

That afternoon, it seemed Grinder had a lot to get off his chest.

He went on: 'Listen, there were other coppers much higher-ranked than me who'd sanction things that would make your hair curl. But I wasn't involved in any of that shit. I was a fuckin' top thief-taker for Chrissake! I knew I'd be judged on results, so I knocked down a few doors. So fuckin' what?'

Grinder rolled his eyes when I then asked him how he could afford such a large home.

'Here we go again,' he muttered. 'So a few sad old coppers have got jealous? I can afford this place because I sold my house in south London for a packet and did some security work for the Saudis after I retired.

'D'you think I'd really be that stupid to buy myself a flashy house and car if it had all been paid for by corrupt money?'

In the late 1990s, Grinder's police bosses introduced a new rule about the handling of informants, which was supposed to help reduce corruption in the police. It didn't work but The Grinder decided it was the right time to leave the force.

He explained: 'We was told we had to log an informant's real name in a book that everyone could see. Well, that was completely out of order. How could I or any half-decent copper expose his or her informant like that?

'Informants were the lifeblood of any copper worth his salt back then. But try telling that to the university kids who've joined up in recent years. Without informants you can't get a steer on crimes that are in the pipeline and prevent them from actually happening. Surely that's the most important aspect of good policing?'

But Grinder did admit he was lucky to get out of the police 'in one piece'.

He told me: 'I was considered an old dinosaur. I wasn't gonna play by the new rules. I did my own thing and I had the results to prove it. But there were these educated types coming through the ranks then for the first time and they thought I was a loose cannon.'

And he had plenty to say about *Line of Duty*: 'It's a load of crap! They make it look as if we're all bent. Look, being a copper is no picnic. Sure, you have to lean on people sometimes and maybe that occasionally involves violence. But *Line of Duty* makes it look as if we're all up to our necks in bribes. Most coppers simply don't have the time or the inclination to get so immersed in corrupt practices.'

Whatever.

Just north of Grinder's sumptuous home on the Costa del Sol resides a retired former detective called Mad Dog, who insisted Grinder was a big-time player when it came to police corruption.

MAD DOG

Mad Dog hadn't met Grinder since they worked together at Scotland Yard, despite living so close to each other in retirement.

Mad Dog told me: 'He [Grinder] is a fucking lucky man! He should have been locked up because of all the corrupt stunts he pulled when we worked together. I always reckoned he had something on our bosses because it seemed as if he was untouchable.

'I remember one time Grinder arrested the teenage son of a notorious Kent drug smuggler and tried to pressurise him into giving evidence against his father. Well, that kid's father went ballistic and charged into our offices screaming blue murder. This villain started shouting his mouth off about a drug deal in London which he claimed had been financed by serving policemen, including The Grinder.

'Well, guess what? That criminal's kid was released a few hours later. The following day, two detectives from another force were ordered to go round and see the same criminal at his home and take a statement under caution about the alleged drug deal connected to Grinder.'

But before the detectives got to the house, their boss received a call from the same villain's lawyer. He told police his client had gone abroad and wouldn't be coming back to the UK in the near future to give evidence against Grinder or anyone else, despite the claims he'd made earlier.

The two detectives didn't even bother interviewing The Grinder because they knew he'd 'got' to that villain.

Mad Dog added: 'Now maybe you'll understand why I don't socialise with Grinder out here in Spain. I've steered clear of him since that incident. He's bad news.'

And then there are the corrupt cops who become the ultimate cold-blooded killers.

THE JACKAL

In Northern Ireland, police corruption seems far more wide-reaching than on the UK mainland, as this book has already highlighted in part when looking at the background of *Line of Duty*'s Ted Hastings.

However, the case of a Northern Irish corrupt policeman who in the 1990s worked as a hitman known as The Jackal stunned police forces across the UK. It was even claimed recently that this psychopathic officer was once commissioned by other corrupt Northern Irish detectives to kill one of his own colleagues.

Some officers were alleged to have suppressed evidence that would have helped investigators confirm that the gunman was their fanatical loyalist colleague Robin Jackson. He worked for British military intelligence *and* the Royal Ulster Constabulary's Special Branch.

Jackson revelled in his nickname The Jackal and was eventually blamed for more than 100 murders of mostly Catholic civilians. He was never brought in for questioning in relation to any of these murders and died of cancer at his home in 1998.

But Jackson's case perfectly illustrates the type of toxic environment *Line of Duty*'s Ted Hastings trained in as a young rookie cop and why he became such a good fit as head of AC-12.

So while Hastings' background undoubtedly plays a pivotal role in helping him crack cases, what about the true crime dilemmas so relevant to the real *Line of Duty*?

Chapter Five

THE REAL STORY

'There's only one thing I'm interested in, and that's catching bent coppers.'
Chief Superintendent Ted Hastings, *Line of Duty*

GOOD OR BAD?

In both *Line of Duty* and the so-called real world, corrupt detectives are talked about in fairly bland black and white terms. They're either good or bad and there is little room for grey as far as most law-abiding officers are concerned.

Not surprisingly, corrupt police officers are considered traitors by many of their colleagues. In *Line of Duty*, the police hammer home this message over and over again, whenever possible. But what happens when guilt-riddled crooked officers decide they want to turn their back on corruption and do the right thing?

As one retired detective explained: 'The hardest thing for

any police officer is to go corrupt and then try to back out of it by helping honest coppers to put other bad cops in jail.' However, without the bravery of those officers prepared to take such risks, many of the most dangerous corrupt cops would never be brought to justice.

'*Line of Duty* sometimes makes it all seem too easy,' one retired Flying Squad detective explained. 'An officer is corrupt and that's it. They throw the book at him and then throw the key away. But corruption is often not as simple as that. Many of the most successful officers I've worked with would be considered corrupt in today's police. But I never saw them as such back in the day.'

He went on: 'Coppers thirty, forty years ago were often obliged to mix with criminals to find out what was happening in the underworld. Sure, they sometimes accepted a drink from those criminals but that didn't mean they were on the take.

'The key to good policing back in those days – especially before police computers and all that stuff came along – was having your nose to the ground, which could even sometimes mean appearing to be corrupt even if you were not. The trouble is that today you'd be condemned as bent without being given a chance to explain. That is bad for on-the-ground policing and it is watering down our ability to bring the bad guys to justice.'

And there is also another side to this vexed question of good and bad cops, which *Line of Duty* itself has started to deal with in recent series.

The same retired Flying Squad detective explained:

'Sometimes as a police officer you genuinely have to pretend to be corrupt to get inside a criminal organisation. That used to happen quite a lot, but these days, there are so many rules and regulations about handling criminals that most serving coppers are afraid to operate in this way.

'Back in the 1990s, I personally had to "take a bribe" from a criminal in order to discover the details of a massive drug haul coming into the UK. The criminals themselves saw it as a test to make sure I was not a straight copper. If I'd hesitated, my cover would have been blown and my life would have been put in danger.

'Today, that sort of operation just wouldn't happen and all those drugs would have got into the UK and poisoned many young people.'

UK's security services MI5 and MI6 regularly use serving police officers, as well as their own agents, to infiltrate criminal organisations. And that can also mean pretending to accept bribes.

Another former detective recalled: 'In one case I know of, the family of an undercover cop had to be seen even spending the money he'd been paid in a bribe to convince criminals that he was not an undercover cop. How would that be possible in today's police forces?'

But on the other hand, as one recently retired detective explained: 'Taking a bribe might or might not be the only way to enable an undercover cop to infiltrate a criminal organisation. But it's also a very convenient way for a real crooked cop to operate.

'A lot of today's coppers simply don't accept so many of

those "grey rules" when it comes to corruption. Surely that's a good thing? Let's be frank, back in the day, many more police officers were getting away with corrupt practices than they are today.'

POINT OF THE CIRCLE

Police forces across the UK and Western Europe contain many members of the Freemasons. It's even been rumoured that affiliated police chiefs across the continent have launched clandestine operations to wipe out criminals in deadly, cross-border conspiracies that defy the common rule of law. *Line of Duty*'s plotlines have occasionally touched upon the controversial connections between the police and the Freemasons. There is even a clear hint that AC-12 boss Ted Hastings is a member.

Those outside the Freemasons consider it a mysterious and secretive organisation. But members themselves insist it is a society of men concerned with moral and spiritual values. As one police officer – who is not a Freemason – told me: 'I've always been highly sceptical about police officers being Freemasons. But obviously it's a free world and they have a right to be a member of any club they wish. But it does bother a lot of officers who are not members.'

Those outside the Freemasons' tainted circle have alleged that some of its police-affiliated members have used corruption to control their colleagues in law enforcement across the UK.

I've come across numerous examples of intriguing connections between some Freemason cops and a number of notorious British criminals.

It's clear that some gangsters have joined the Freemasons in order to get closer to members. How much power and influence they wield through this country's politicians and lawmakers will probably never be known, but professional criminals know full well that being a member is very useful for their type of 'business'.

In the early 1980s, some of south-east England's richest professional criminals joined one particular Freemasons' lodge through an introduction via a well-known Kent criminal, who'd been nurturing Freemason police officers for years.

Many years later, two former detectives told me that membership applications by these same criminals were proposed and seconded by serving police officers, who wanted to have such influential villains 'onside'.

There have also been allegations that members of the Brink's-Mat heist gang and other professional criminals 'infiltrated' the Freemasons, both before and after the heist, back in November 1983. It was alleged they'd also been supported for membership by police officers.

Some police members of one Freemason lodge near London – which a number of professional criminals joined in the late 1970s – were so outraged, they quit the organisation. But others believed that having criminals as members was an opportunity to pick up good informants.

Other Freemason members of that same lodge near London included gold bullion dealers from Hatton Garden, as well as other serving policemen, judges and even lawyers.

When one notorious criminal appeared in court in south-east London in the 1990s, detectives became highly suspicious of the presence of a Freemason-connected officer. The villain was on trial for a number of offences, including importation of a firearm and fraud. He was very lucky to get a suspended prison sentence plus a £2,500 fine. Many believe to this day that the criminal's crooked police friends helped him avoid a jail sentence.

A number of powerful UK criminals are even renowned for using a Freemasons' handshake, which involves putting the thumb between the first and second finger and pressing the knuckle on the middle finger. This would indicate that the person in question was 'on the square' – Mason-speak for being a member. Whenever such criminals met a police officer, they'd make a point of using the handshake very carefully to ascertain his or her membership.

One retired detective – who witnessed one of these exchanges – later explained: 'The moment the Freemasons were mentioned, this villain was allowed to leave with no charges being pressed. There was only one reason that happened.'

On another occasion, a senior police detective investigating a notorious robbery interrogated a suspect about his involvement in the crime. The criminal tried a Masonic handshake on the officer, followed by an offer of a £1 million bribe for 'help' re the charge. The officer immediately reported the approach to his supervisors at Scotland Yard.

As one retired Freemason detective later pointed out: 'There have been many of these sort of incidents between officers and suspects but most of them are never actually reported to anyone.'

Another former Flying Squad detective explained: 'We all

know that villains join the Masons to get close to the police. But remember, it works both ways because many officers want these sorts of connections because it can help them catch the bad guys.

'The main problem is that corrupt officers are also members of the Masons and that is a bitter pill to swallow because the Masons are supposed to be a fine, upstanding institution beyond reproach.'

There are no signs that either the Freemasons or the UK underworld are planning to overhaul their involvement with each other any time soon.

THE DOME JOB

There can occasionally be some unlikely 'bonuses' for the police, thanks to their two-timing corrupt colleagues. One corrupt cop who was working for a notorious gang of robbers actually helped prevent one of the UK's biggest ever armed heists from happening when he decided to turn against his underworld paymasters.

This all happened back in November 2000 – seventeen years after the Brink's-Mat heist had blown open a vast network of crooked cops.

A gang of professional criminals from south-east England decided to target the Millennium Dome, in Greenwich, London. They planned to steal a huge diamond on display inside the Dome. It was said to be worth in the region of £200 million.

The gang even paid the aforementioned corrupt officer for

information about the location of cameras and other security measures at the robbery location.

The detective in question was so torn when he realised the enormity of what he was doing that he took a huge risk and admitted his corrupt relationship in order to keep his law-abiding police colleagues informed. It was just days before the gang intended to steal that diamond from the Dome.

Detectives immediately mounted a finely tuned surveillance operation, knowing they could not arrest any of the suspects on serious charges until they actually began the robbery.

On 7 November 2000, a bulldozer driven by one member of the gang rammed into fencing surrounding the Dome. Dozens of armed detectives swarmed around the robbers and they were all arrested.

The identity of the corrupt detective who turned informant to help prevent the robbery has never been revealed for obvious reasons.

As one retired south London officer explained: 'They might well have had him killed if they'd known what he'd done. That was a very difficult investigation for police because we didn't like having to support an officer who'd admitted he was corrupt. But in fairness, he did do the right thing in the end, so hats off to him.'

The same detective added: 'He later said he'd never intended to become a bent cop. He got pulled into it by peer pressure from two older detectives, who'd been on the take for years.'

And that peer pressure can come from all directions.

UK'S NARCO COPS

Line of Duty's creator Jed Mercurio has cleverly woven powerful narratives through all the series of this drama while at the same time focusing on one big dramatic thread per series. It's a clever ploy to keep people watching and satisfy their demands as an audience.

But in the real world, police corruption is not so easy to 'bring to justice' within a particular time period. And there is one criminal activity above all else which has helped fuel corruption within the UK police.

Towards the end of the 1970s, many former bank and security van robbers turned to the drug business because the profits were much larger and the risks minimal compared to 'going across the pavement', as such raids were called back then.

As a result of this, a more sophisticated type of corrupt officer emerged. He (or she) discovered there was less risk and much larger cash returns to be made by working for so-called top-end drug barons. These same crooked officers even proved to be shrewd investors in straight businesses, using their own proceeds from crime. Others even laundered cash as well.

The immense earning potential of drugs changed the face of police corruption over the final two decades of the last century. Criminals were prepared to 'invest' in having the sharpest crooked officers on their payroll. But, typically, they didn't trust most people, so they kept their gangs small and compact. Again, this was good news for bent cops because it meant there was less chance of them being 'grassed up' to their honest colleagues.

As a result, most of these shady underworld shenanigans remained largely hidden from public view and steeped in intrigue. At Scotland Yard, there was still a reluctance to openly refer to police corruption because it was deemed as damaging to the police as a whole.

While the armed robbers of the previous criminal era were upfront and 'in yer face', drug barons and their two-faced corrupt police officer friends were the complete opposite. Together, they lurked in the shadows, subtly terrorising enemies and colleagues alike.

In south-east England, there were renegade gangs of crooked officers notorious for taking a cut from every drug haul they came across. One former drug squad detective explained: 'I know it sounds like something you'd only come across in Mexico or Colombia but it happens here too. Drugs are still the biggest motivation when it comes to police corruption.'

The UK police themselves are reluctant to provide specific figures, but it's believed that tens of millions of pounds' worth of drugs have been 'confiscated' by corrupt officers. Those drugs were then either sold to other criminal gangs, or officers set up their own 'dealerships' to sell narcotics on the open market. Often, they also kept aside some for their own personal use.

The same officer added: 'That's the power of drugs for you. There is so much money involved that everyone – including the bent cops – wants a cut of either the cash or the "produce".'

And we're not just talking about corrupt police officers here, either. For the right price, judges, even politicians, can be 'bought off' to provide essential inside information and influence so that drug barons can keep one step ahead of their enemies.

Some police officers insist that many criminals like to boast openly about these sorts of connections because they want to taint their old enemies, the police and the Establishment, by implying they're all 'crooked'. Another former drugs squad officer told me: 'It's an old excuse. The police have always responded like that in relation to any corruption allegations for many years. It's a very effective way of pushing the subject under the carpet.'

In recent years, US-style organised crime gangs centred around the drug trade have started to emerge in this country. These wealthy criminals were even more good news for corrupt officers because they were prepared to pay out even larger bribes.

Today, corrupt police officers' illicit cash is still largely invested in legitimate businesses including pubs, restaurants, clubs and even 'car fronts', otherwise known as open-air used-car lots. Many crooked cops regularly dip in and out of the UK's lucrative property market, often using 'legit' nominees to front up their purchases.

A few years back, one well-known London property dealer went into such a business partnership with a corrupt police detective. They used drug money to invest in office blocks across the capital. But that property developer allegedly ended up owing £600,000 to the bent cop. The businessman eventually 'fell off' the balcony of one of those high-rise offices...

THE COLOMBIANS

Colombian cocaine cartels from Medellín and Cali changed the face of the UK underworld for ever from the mid-1980s onwards. The Colombians brought with them a new attitude towards police corruption. They considered crooked officers to be an essential ingredient in their operation because back in South America, most police were paid bribes as a matter of course and they presumed it would be no different in the UK and Western Europe.

The most famous Narco of all was, of course, Pablo Escobar. Back in the late 1980s, he recognised that the UK and Europe were about to become prime market places for his product. Escobar was determined to organise an efficient supply network, so his cocaine could be sold in the UK with ease.

As a professional old-school British criminal source of mine explained: 'Escobar reckoned he could get himself a big slice of all the British and European profits if he sent his people over to start running cartel regional offices in cities like London and Madrid.'

Some of Britain and Europe's most legendary professional criminals – including ex-Great Train Robber Charlie Wilson – had become drug barons by the late 1980s. But they soon found out how brutal the Colombian suppliers could be and a number of them – including Wilson – were murdered by hitmen paid by Escobar.

Meanwhile, corrupt police officers – many of whom had helped the first wave of old-school British drug barons – were left to sink or swim.

Escobar's first representative in London was a woman known only as 'La Patrona' (lady boss) in the UK underworld. She was rumoured to have ordered the killing of at least two 'troublesome' crooked UK police officers after setting up the Medellín cartel's London office in 1990.

'Both of them were killed by hitmen on the back of motorbikes,' my source explained. 'Of course it's a classic South American way to knock off people, so it sent a message to all of us – including other bent coppers – not to consider informing on them to the police or else.'

Escobar even ordered his London representative to put a number of corrupt police officers in the south-east of England on retainers because he recognised their importance to the success of his UK operation. The Colombians believed they could turn cities like London and Madrid into European versions of Medellín and Cali.

Today, police officers from that era recall in hushed tones the fear and trepidation they felt when it became clear the South American cartels were running their drug networks from inside the UK.

The shooting dead of Narco King Pablo Escobar by security forces in 1993 in his hometown of Medellín made no difference, either. His Medellín cartel had dozens working for La Patrona in London. In Madrid, at least 3,000 Colombians were employed via the cartels by the mid-1990s.

In the UK, some renegade corrupt police officers were working virtually full-time for Colombian drug cartels and being paid hundreds of thousands of pounds each to guarantee that the supply of cocaine from South America could reach UK shores virtually uninterrupted.

One former south London detective explained: 'The Colombians owned a lot of coppers back then. Their fingerprints were on every aspect of the cocaine business in the UK. We knew it was happening but there was a reluctance on the part of senior police officers and politicians to get involved because there was so little info on them and this made law enforcement seem weak and ineffective.'

Ironically, back in Colombia, the two main Cali and Medellín cartels were finally starting to be dismantled by the DEA and local security forces. In the UK, Escobar's beloved La Patrona was about to cut and run from Europe when she was arrested for murdering a young lover and ended up serving a long sentence in a UK prison.

The Colombians then opted for a cut from every load of cocaine to reach UK shores, but their direct involvement in selling the drug in this country was over.

Another former south London drug squad officer explained: 'It must have been a big relief to those corrupt officers being paid by the Colombians because they pulled out without trying to silence all their bent coppers. But the sad thing is that we were never able to bring most of them to justice as a result.'

The Colombians had left a vacuum that would end up being filled by gangs of even more ruthless criminals, who'd eventually nurture a new generation of corrupt police officers.

THE NEW INVADERS

From 2000 onwards, immigrant gangsters began flooding into the UK. This influx of mainly Eastern European criminals would eventually set the war against corrupt cops back many years.

The Balkan gangs were prepared to handle all the drugs the Colombians, Moroccans and the world's other narco states could supply them with and the UK was a much-prized marketplace.

One former drug squad officer told me: 'These Eastern Europeans had nothing to lose. Many of them had just come out of a vicious war, so selling coke in Western Europe and the UK was low-risk for them.'

These gangs comprised mainly of Albanian criminals, whose history going back hundreds of years had always revolved around smuggling contraband from the East to the West.

The UK police didn't have a clue who most of them were because they used false identification documents and travelled back and forth between the Balkans and the UK almost on a weekly basis. This gave these gangs virtually a free run at the drugs trade in this country.

Albanian and other Eastern European gangs quickly set up their distribution hubs in many of the UK's major cities. 'It was easy pickings for them because they were prepared to get their fingers dirty, unlike the young British criminals who were trying to get into the drugs game at that time,' explained my criminal source.

These mainly Albanian gangs now based in the UK's major

cities then began an active 'recruitment campaign' for corrupt UK police officers. The narco balance of power was swinging in their favour and they needed bent coppers to help them consolidate their powerbase in the UK.

My source further explained: 'The Albanians were good at picking up bent coppers to work for them. These officers soon began arresting any criminals not approved by the Albanians. The Balkan lads wanted all the other villains out of the big cities, so they could run everything themselves.'

As a result, the druglands of most of the big cities in the UK continue to be run by those Eastern European gangs to this day. They often use youths and even children to sell their 'produce' on the city streets. Crooked cops are a vital part of their business operation and many are paid monthly retainers. These ruthless Balkan gangsters like to boast about them, too.

One recently retired London drug squad detective told me: 'The Albanian mafia claimed recently they've got a number of senior police officers in London and the south-east of England on their payroll.

'One crooked officer I nicked just before I retired said the Albanians were ruthless but actually much better to work for than the Colombians or even the old-school Brits. Apparently, the Albanians always pay their corrupt police officers on time and treat them as proper work colleagues, rather than with the contempt that used to be shown to them by British criminals back in the day.'

The same former detective recalled: 'In the old days, you could often work out who the corrupt coppers and their criminal handlers were. But today it's much harder with these Eastern European gangs. Often, we don't even know the real names of these criminals and neither do the corrupt police officers who are working for them.'

Many real-life detectives I've spoken to say they'd like to see *Line of Duty* feature more of the 'reality' of the foreign gangs 'epidemic' that has swept through the UK in recent years. But they also recognise this is a highly complex issue.

Another retired detective said: 'These foreign gangs are running the drugs underworld in the UK today. The British criminals are scared of them and hardly know any of the Balkan gangsters by name, so they can't even trade them off to the police. It's a win-win situation for the Eastern Europeans, which doesn't look likely to change any time soon.'

As well, Eastern European gangsters even have crooked customs officers they 'own' in major ports across the country on their payroll.

NO SMOKE WITHOUT FIRE

There is clear evidence that cannabis has had a bigger long-term impact on police corruption in the UK than many would realise. Hash barons I've interviewed down the years have openly admitted that corrupt cops are often the key to their success when it comes to this multi-million pound criminal enterprise.

For hash still provides one of the biggest single sources of actual illicit income for organised crime gangs across the UK. But law enforcers have failed in recent years to eradicate it from our streets because the police have had to prioritise so-called harder drugs, such as cocaine and heroin.

Meanwhile, the cannabis business has gone from strength to strength, with corrupt police officers playing a crucial role working for criminal organisations that produce and then import the drug into this lucrative marketplace.

Some police officers believe that large numbers of corrupt police officers have joined forces with cannabis gangs in recent years because it's not considered as criminally tainted as other, more powerful drugs businesses. One retired detective explained: 'Some of my workmates smoked hash and they looked on it as being softer and less harmful than coke and E and other drugs, not to mention alcohol. And I believe this has convinced them that there's nothing wrong with taking a bribe now and again from a pot gang.

'Of course, they're sadly misguided. The same gangs invariably often deal in Class A drugs, and in any case, if something is illegal, it's illegal full stop.'

A few years back, I interviewed a British hash baron called Fred, who ran his criminal activities out of southern Spain. He smuggled hash over from the Atlas Mountains in Morocco.

Fred also happened to be a former Home Counties police detective. He recalled: 'I had all the UK contacts. I had serving cops back in the UK and a couple of retired detectives out here working for me. I worked on the premise that if they were crooked cops then they'd be much more loyal to me because they wouldn't want to risk their pensions.'

Fred revealed that his entire operation fell apart when the

Spanish police – the Guardia Civil – raided his warehouse near Malaga, where he was storing £5 million worth of hash. 'I wasn't there, so I managed to avoid arrest but I couldn't understand how the Spanish cops found out about the warehouse in the first place.'

Then one of the ex-cops Fred was employing disappeared without trace, only to turn up a year later in Thailand.

Fred explained: 'I later heard this ex-cop had traded in my hash business to the Spanish police to stop himself being deported back to the UK to face corruption charges. I should have known better. You can't trust a cop, even a bent one. In fact, they're the worst of the lot.'

THE MONEY TRAIL

Today, many inside Britain's police forces are pushing to introduce New York-style so-called 'zero tolerance' on all aspects of corruption inside UK law enforcement. 'The trouble is that could end up with a lot of innocent officers being hounded when they've done nothing wrong,' one recently retired detective pointed out.

The UK's Revenue and Customs officials plus the National Crime Agency have even recently set up specialist units to try and monitor organised-crime gangs, flagged up for having corrupt police officers on their books. But the results have so far been very limited.

'The trouble is that we could end up with a lot of innocent officers being hounded when they've done nothing wrong,' one recently retired detective pointed out.

But on the other hand, there is clear evidence that many other corrupt officers are slipping through the net.

An influx of mainly Eastern European gangs into the UK's drug trade in recent years has made exposing crooked cops even harder. The same recently retired detective explained: 'In the old days, bent coppers and their criminal pals often had something linking them together from their pasts.

'But today, these foreign gangs simply recruit police officers with no previous connections to them. That makes it even harder to expose them. As a result, we now probably know even less about what corrupt officers are up to than we did twenty or thirty years ago. It doesn't bode well for the future.'

And within many police departments across the UK there is an inbuilt fear of questioning an officer's honesty without having extremely strong evidence to support such accusations. One retired detective explained: 'Some coppers are just plain nasty but that doesn't make them corrupt. Trouble is, some officers get bullied by others and then start throwing unfounded accusations around and that is very damaging to everyone.'

Meanwhile, in the UK underworld itself, most criminals are extremely reluctant to inform on bent police officers. 'That can come back to haunt you,' explained one retired bank robber from south London. 'Professional criminals know what side their bread is buttered. They don't want to rock the boat and they want to keep their bent coppers onside.'

Another problem is that crooked officers' associates will do everything in their power to force a criminal to retract corrupt cop allegations on the basis that they're simply smearing an officer because of a personal grudge.

That clouds the issue even further and often ends up being used by lawyers to successfully defend corrupt officers.

No wonder the shady 'netherworld' of police criminality knows no bounds.

CLEAN SKIN

Line of Duty's dramatic structure means that it usually follows its main characters in 'real time' with virtually no flashbacks. This enables the audience to stay with the story as it unfolds.

But there is often a need to go back to one corrupt officer's route to criminality from when he first signed up for the force. For there is no doubt that crooked cops sometimes deliberately join the police on the orders of their gangster bosses.

In police terminology these characters are referred to as 'clean skins' – individuals with no existing criminal record who would therefore not have attracted the attention of police or security forces in their youth.

In series five of *Line of Duty*, such a character ended up killing Detective Inspector John Corbett to prevent a spider's web of corruption from being exposed. In real life, such 'clean skin' cases are just as chilling.

In 2006, Mesut Karakas was just nineteen years old when he decided to join London's Metropolitan Police. But what no one realised at the time was that he'd been nurtured by his childhood friends into becoming a dirty cop from day one. As such, he was paid to be their 'eyes and ears'.

So Karakas was the perfect 'clean skin'.

As one recently retired officer explained: 'Increasing

numbers of these types of characters have been joining the police in recent years. It's very worrying because there's no way of knowing about their criminal connections because they have "clean skins".'

In 2010, Karakas was unmasked as a crooked officer when police planted a listening device in his car. The bug planted by the Yard's anti-corruption investigators revealed every detail of a plot to kidnap a bank manager in front of his family and force him to hand over cash, and detectives were able to move in on Karakas and his gang of criminal associates before they'd even reached the bank manager's house.

Ironically, the bent cop, now twenty-four, was even heard by a police surveillance listening device discussing a TV show centred around exactly the same type of operation. Karakas even referred to the 'golden rule' of the underworld, which is never to talk openly about criminal activities in case they're being monitored.

Detectives listened avidly as Karakas spoke about what the gang would do to their bank manager target and his family. One of them was heard asking: 'Will the female scream?' They even talked about setting aside ninety minutes to make the bank manager co-operate in full. The five men also referred to staging a roadworks scene near the victim's home as a distraction for the kidnap.

When officers raided the property where the crime was being planned, they uncovered false registration plates, industrial gaffer tape, dust masks, a balaclava, plasti-cuffs, industrial ear protectors and a van which was to be used for the getaway.

'We heard them planning the route, what time they should

commit the offence, when there would be less police on the street and what CCTV cameras would be looking at them,' one detective later recalled. 'There was clearly a real chance of violence being perpetrated. The victims would have their mouths taped over and hands tied and people with balaclavas would be coming through their door.'

The police swooped before the gang could inflict harm on their kidnap victim.

After Karakas' arrest, it emerged that he'd been encouraged to join the police by former school friends, who'd formed an independent gang of criminals. And then it was revealed that Karakas had already been investigated about alleged links to two major drug dealers and Turkish organised crime gangsters in north London. Doubt about his character had even been raised by colleagues back in 2007, three years before he was brought to justice. This came amid suspicions that he had injured himself with scissors in order to frame a suspect.

Not long after this incident, Karakas and his criminal associates launched a vicious baseball attack on a man outside a pub in Islington, north London. The following day, Karakas took down details of the investigation from the police computer. Bribes and threats were made to the victim to drop the charges.

However, police have never explained why they ignored these obvious red flags about Karakas' character. The former detective explained: 'The Karakas case is very troubling because there is a clear implication that his troubled past was ignored, even though it was clearly a warning sign about his corrupt activities.

'The obvious conclusion is that other officers were covering up for him. There is no actual concrete proof of this but it looks very suspicious.'

Other police officers have a much simpler explanation: 'In this politically correct day and age many officers are reluctant to throw corruption allegations at their colleagues, especially if they're from a minority group, as was the case with Karakas. That can help the bad guys like him to manipulate the situation and it's often too late by the time we find out what they're really up to.'

Karakas eventually pleaded guilty at Blackfriars Crown Court to assault, conspiracy to kidnap and misconduct in public office. He was sentenced to thirteen years imprisonment.

But the case continues to spark serious questions.

'We all want to know how he managed to even last four years in the police, considering he was committing crimes virtually from the first day he joined,' said one recently retired detective.

Police corruption is fuelled by a surprisingly vast range of criminal enterprises.But how do corrupt cops deal with the inevitable con-sequences of their actions once they've been exposed?

BANGED UP

Line of Duty hasn't really dealt with the full-scale, harsh reality of what happens to corrupt police officers when they're imprisoned. There is a presumption that they'll face multiple physical and sexual assaults by other inmates because of an inbuilt hatred of so-called 'boys in blue'.

But like everything connected to bent coppers, nothing is ever as it appears on the surface.

'Speedy' is the nickname of a crooked Home Counties detective who received one of the longest-ever jail terms for police corruption.

Speedy dreaded being sent to prison. After all, he was the ultimate 'enemy' in the eyes of other inmates. He'd heard stories about how inmates put glass and excrement in food, urinated in beds and handed out vicious punishments in the showers.

Even the prison officers who escorted Speedy to jail after his conviction felt sorry for him. One of them gave him some sound advice: 'Don't let them see the fear in your eyes, son. Ignore them, but do it with a steely expression on your face.'

Speedy entered prison following his conviction with a nervous shrug of his shoulders, believing that it was inevitable he was about to enter hell on earth. 'I'd even heard a rumour before my sentencing in court that a villain whom I'd accepted bribes from had paid an inmate in this same prison to murder me,' he recalled. 'He wanted to ensure I never told the police about his activities even though I'd been careful not to inform on him for obvious reasons. But he didn't seem to believe I'd keep quiet.'

But let's go back to that first day inside. Speedy continued: 'I took on board what the prison officers had told me and decided to try and tough it out.'

Within ten minutes of arriving in his cell, a small, wiry inmate entered and greeted Speedy in a very over-friendly way, which made him even more paranoid. Speedy explained:

'But I kept calm and quickly worked out he must have been sent into my cell to see how I was handling it. This was, in effect, my audition. So I puffed myself up, smiled coldly and told him I was looking forward to meeting all the other chaps on my landing.'

Then the same inmate leaned in close and whispered: 'There's a few out there who'd like to kick the shit out of you but you'll be fine, mate.'

Speedy recalled: 'Instead of melting down and looking terrified, I grabbed this little ferret by the scruff of his collar and said, "Tell 'em to come and see me and I'll sort 'em out." It was madness really, but I knew if I didn't play hard from the get-go then I'd become the inmates' human pin cushion.'

Meanwhile, the same snaky inmate disappeared down the prison corridor to pass on Speedy's message. He never heard another thing that night.

The following morning in the canteen, Speedy sat on his own, deliberately.

He explained: 'Then these three real hard nut types plonked themselves down right opposite and next to me. I didn't even look up at them. Then one of them slapped me on the back and smiled. "You're gonna be fine in here, squire."

'I looked him straight in the eyes and said, "Why wouldn't I be fine in here, squire?"'

Speedy recalled: 'Instead of kicking off, he and his two friends started chatting ten to the dozen about everything from their families to football. It seemed I'd passed their test with flying colours.'

From that day on, Speedy says he was always treated with the utmost respect inside prison. 'In a strange sort of way, I'd earned respect from them because they realised I was nothing more than just another criminal like them, if that makes any sense.'

And the alleged hitman plot to kill Speedy inside prison never materialised, either. And soon he was running various 'activities' on his wing, including handing out free legal advice and running a book group.

'The prison officers were happy to let me do all this because they saw me as a calming influence amongst some very volatile inmates,' said Speedy. 'I learned so much about myself inside prison. I'd been a wreck of a character while I was a copper on the take and now I was slowly recovering my confidence. You realise inside prison that everyone deserves a second chance in life.

'Some of those inmates could have killed or maimed me but they were willing to let me start with a clean slate.'

But in the real outside world, some corrupt cops can't handle the heat, so they head for the hills.

BOLTHOLES

Line of Duty's excellent storylines make gripping television because they so often accurately reflect the real world of modern policing, as well as injecting many of the same domestic problems most of us face during our lifetime. This virtually guarantees the audience can relate easily to these characters.

But unlike many of us in the so-called 'normal world', criminals and bent coppers have a habit of running away to another country when they're about to be cornered. One of their favourite destinations is Northern Cyprus. My connections to this sparsely populated Mediterranean hinterland go back more than twenty years to the early summer of 1997 when I was hunting runaway criminals from the Brink's-Mat heist for a book and TV documentary about the robbery.

Northern Cyprus is a strangely unwelcoming Turkish-run bolthole. No doubt much of this is down to the fact there was (and still is) no extradition treaty with the UK. This all makes it the perfect destination for those who need to 'keep a low profile', as they say in the underworld.

It's said that today there are more British villains on the north side of this partitioned island than anywhere else in the world, apart from Spain's notorious Costa del Crime and Thailand. But what isn't so well known is that a handful of corrupt UK police officers have also quietly 'retired' to this lawless territory over the past twenty-five years.

Former detective Foxy chose to settle in Northern Cyprus in the early 1990s when he left the UK 'in a hurry' after senior officers forced him into early retirement.

Perhaps not surprisingly, Foxy wasn't very helpful when I first turned up at his half-built villa on a swelteringly hot morning in May 1997. 'No comment,' were the only words he uttered in response when I introduced myself. When I pressed him further, he produced a baseball bat from behind the front door and said: 'Time to fuck off, mate. I ain't helping you.'

Moments later, Foxy completely changed his mind and invited me in. I have no idea why to this day.

'I don't want people knowing I'm here,' Foxy told me over a cup of tea, a few minutes later. 'I know what people were saying about me back home. I admit I took a few risks but I never helped a villain wriggle out of charges or anything like that. I just tipped him the nod now and again if he was being watched. That was it, I swear.'

I later learned that Foxy had settled in Northern Cyprus after he joined forces with an old-school British professional criminal on the island to launch a holiday letting business. It never got off the ground.

But I was told by one of Foxy's former colleagues back in the UK that his business partner was the same criminal he'd been accused of helping before he left the UK police.

Foxy's former colleague later explained: 'Foxy took the money and ran – literally. In many ways I don't blame him. Everyone here hated his guts and Northern Cyprus is the sort of place where you can do what you like without any interference from the state.'

Other former police officers and criminals who have tried to settle on Northern Cyprus have not been so lucky. One member of a gang that pulled off one of the biggest cash robberies of recent years turned up here while on the run from the police, back in the UK. He 'disappeared' a few days after he was first spotted.

Another crooked British police officer who turned up on the island about ten years ago is also said to have 'gone missing' and was never seen again.

It often feels as if no amount of money can make it worth-while becoming a corrupt police officer.

But some might disagree…

SLOW BURNER

Obviously, the cleverest corrupt police officers are the ones who never get caught. In the fictional world of *Line of Duty*, the 'rules' of television drama mean the bad cops usually have to be brought to justice in the end. But during many years investigating the real underworld, I've come across corrupt police officers of all sizes and shapes and backgrounds who've never been caught.

Bunter grew up in the slums of postwar Birmingham alongside a school friend, who went on to become one of the UK's richest-ever villains.

Despite joining the police, he always kept in touch with his old pal. As Bunter told me many years later: 'When we were teenagers, I used to try and get him to give up being a villain but I soon realised it was a lost cause. Then he went off and made a fortune from handling stolen goods before opening a dodgy holiday business in the sunshine.'

Bunter kept in touch with his friend throughout and for years, they even agreed a golden rule never to discuss either of their 'jobs'. He often went to stay at his criminal friend's mansion at a Mediterranean resort: 'I didn't see anything wrong with that because we never mentioned anything about crime. I even told my bosses that it was important to keep close to him in any case.'

Then about twenty years ago that relationship changed for ever. Bunter explained: 'I was staying at his place in the sunshine and we went out clubbing and met some ladies. It all got a bit crazy. I ended up getting hammered with him and naturally, the ladies stayed overnight.'

The next day, Bunter's criminal friend took him out for lunch and asked him for some inside information about another criminal. 'I said no way,' explained Bunter.

Bunter's friend immediately apologised.

'But he started treating me differently from that moment onwards,' recalled Bunter. 'I felt uncomfortable and he even pointed out that most coppers would presume I was bent because I was close to him, in any case. He had a point when he said that, but I chose not to respond immediately.'

All the time the question of being bribed for information kept going round and round inside Bunter's head. 'Then I thought, what the hell? No one would know what I was up to and he was offering me thousands of pounds just for a bit of info about some unimportant minor league villain.'

But a few days after Bunter got back to the UK he became so overcome with guilt, he told his police bosses what he'd done. 'I was sure I could convince them that I only agreed to help this villain to get closer to him, which could then help us bring a lot of bad guys to justice.'

But Bunter's police bosses did not agree. They'd already suspected he was corrupt and now they were convinced he was.

'I was distraught,' he explained. 'Then my boss said he'd give me one more chance. But I'd have to stick close to my old criminal mate because they wanted me to pump him for information about a number of unsolved crimes he'd been connected to.'

Bunter didn't realise that his multi-millionaire criminal friend already had Bunter's police boss in his pocket. 'It was all a test and I'd failed at the first hurdle because I wasn't supposed to tell them my old mate wanted me on his payroll.'

But Bunter admitted that discovering his own boss was corrupt made him more inclined to go 'bent' himself. 'I thought, "What the fuck" and started taking bribes. The strange thing is that after I made that decision, I felt a lot happier.'

He eventually went on to become his old schoolmate's favourite corrupt cop.

Bunter explained: 'He showed me much more loyalty than my old boss. He said he'd never grass me up because we'd known each other for so long and I believed him. After all, it was in his interests to keep me safe.'

His childhood pal also agreed never to tell Bunter's crooked boss about their arrangement.

Bunter claims he earned more than a million pounds in bribes from his old criminal friend without ever being exposed. He explained: 'I was very careful, I hid all the money. I didn't spend a penny until long after I retired.'

Bunter died in 2018 of natural causes, without ever having been exposed as a bent copper.

But others were not so fortunate.

BITTER AND TWISTED

One of my closest police sources over the past twenty years is a one-time corrupt detective we'll call Dent, who says he's turned over a completely new leaf since serving time in prison for accepting bribes from professional criminals.

Dent claims he experienced a lot of brutal violence at the hands of his fellow officers after he was originally arrested for corruption.

He explained: 'There was this one old-school detective who had it in for me, big-time. He called me a Judas and had to be dragged off me when I was arrested in front of my family inside my own home.'

As Dent was being taken by car to a police station, this same officer ordered the driver to pull up. Then he dragged Dent out of the vehicle and beat the living daylights out of him. Two other officers present turned and looked away. They never once tried to pull the officer off Dent.

Dent later explained: 'I stayed passive, curled up in a ball on the ground and just let him hit and kick me over and over again. The odd thing is it felt as if I deserved it all.'

A few days later, Dent's wife met the same detective's wife in a local supermarket in the suburban neighbourhood where they all lived. Dent recalled: 'She told my wife that her husband had had a nervous breakdown shortly after he arrested me for corruption'.

It turned out he was juggling two mistresses as well as his family and one of those women was blackmailing him. She turned out to be the wife of a local gangster. 'No wonder he had it in for me,' Dent said. 'I must have represented everything he feared he would one day become.'

Since coming out of prison, Dent has got himself a full-time job and turned his back on all forms of crime. He had this advice for any real-life police corruption investigators who might read this book:

'Make sure your home life is calm and "clean". Go to see a therapist if you think everything is falling apart. If you allow all the bad stuff to catch up with you, you'll end up either in a ditch somewhere or smashing someone to death.'

But on the other side, there are certain immensely rich and powerful criminals who consider police corruption a 'tax' well worth paying for.

NO MORE EXCUSES

Are some police officers destined to turn corrupt? Through its excellent storylines *Line of Duty* provides a fascinating insight into what makes police officers become corrupt. But in the real world do any of those excuses make any sense?

One detective explained: 'A lot of us are sick of hearing all the excuses for coppers turning bent. Sure, some of them get caught up in drugs, drink and women and that often leads to their downfall. But there are also some corrupt cops who had a crooked mentality from the day they were born.

'I worked with one constable who was so dishonest he couldn't even walk past a fruit and veg shop without nicking an apple for himself. We all laughed about it at first, but a police officer should not behave in that way.

'The guy himself tried to make out that he only did it so that he could more clearly understand the criminal mind and that made him a better, more efficient copper. And at first we all fell for it. When the finger of suspicion was pointed at him following a claim by an informant that this copper was on the take, we ignored it on the basis it was too obvious! How could he possibly be so blatant?'

The officer continued: 'It wasn't until nearly two years after the rumours first surfaced that this bent cop got caught red-handed. It turned out he'd invested a lot of the money he'd made from bribes in a massage parlour!

'In some ways it was laughable. How could he possibly have thought he could get away with it? At first, this crooked officer claimed he was using the massage parlour to lure criminals in so he could find out what they were up to. But that didn't really wash because he was channelling all the profits from the business into a secret bank account in the Channel Islands.

'In the end, he was brought down, and rightly so.'

But the point about this crooked officer and many others is that some really cannot help themselves. Just because they're police officers doesn't make them any better people than the rest of us.

If that is true then police corruption will probably never be completely stamped out.

And then there is the new group of thoroughly modern crooked police officers, who seem harmless on the surface but have very specific skills which make them immensely 'bribable'.

SUPERGRASSES – 2020-STYLE

Back in the 1970s, when the term 'supergrass' was first used in the media, it referred to criminals informing on their associates. But these days it's also used to describe police officers who inform on their allegedly crooked colleagues.

It's only in recent years that this has even been encouraged.

'A lot of us don't even believe it works,' explained one detective. 'Often, it's an invitation to one corrupt cop to inform on another to get himself off the hook. How can that possibly produce accurate, honest claims?'

As one recently retired detective explained: 'Accusing your colleagues of being bent is a brave move. In many ways it's far more dangerous than when one criminal informs on another. There are some golden unspoken rules inside the police and the number one of these is "Do not grass up yer mates". Until that type of mentality can be stamped out, few corrupt cops will ever be exposed.'

Some serving and recently retired officers genuinely believe that the recruitment of more university-educated police officers is having a positive impact on the supergrass problem. One former detective explained: 'The thinking is that these clever graduate cops will create a failsafe system, which will ensure that any crooked officer offered immunity would have to pass certain "tests" before his testimony was taken seriously.'

But so far there is no evidence that authorities have been any more successful at stamping out police corruption than they were when they started trying to more than two generations ago.

The same detective added: 'They say old habits die hard. Well, police corruption is just like that. Many officers got in the habit and they passed down that mentality to the next generation, who will no doubt do the same thing one day. It is a vicious circle which might never end.

'Corrupt police officers are a very special breed. They're much more artful and deceiving than the rest of us. They have to be because they're taking enormous risks. We're always being told that the introduction of new technology and more advanced scientific areas of policing will eventually help law enforcement to get a proper handle on corruption, but I haven't seen any sign of it so far.'

Recently, one UK police officer who decided to inform on a gang of renegade corrupt detectives found himself enrolled into the witness protection programme because there were real fears that his life was in danger.

One retired detective recalled: 'He told me he wished he'd never stepped forward in the first place. His life and that of his family was turned upside down. The worst aspect of this was that it undoubtedly further put other officers off ever considering informing against their corrupt colleagues, which means most bent cops will remain uncovered.'

COMPUTER GEEKS

To complement the increasingly new modern corrupt practices, the police have had to introduce new ways to sniff out the bent coppers. *Line of Duty* perfectly reflects the reliance of modern policing on computers and so-called new technology. In the real world, it has no doubt also helped the police solve many more crimes. But that in turn has made computer crime itself a much more vulnerable area, especially when it comes to corrupt police officers.

In *Line of Duty*, computer expert officers are seen contributing greatly to the success of anti-corruption operations. PC Maneet Bindra (played by Maya Sondhi)'s new technology skills are vital until she falls into a classic corruption trap. For she is in some ways more vulnerable to corruption than police officers out in the field.

The police's modern-day reliance on computers obviously means that the type of people being recruited by the police has changed drastically. Real-life tech expert officer 'Badger' explained: 'Back in the day, police officers tended to be fairly burly, tough talking characters. There was little room for "the more sensitive souls".'

Today, many more quiet and reserved characters are joining the police and using their skills on computers to help bring criminals to justice. But a lot of these academic-type characters are often much less streetwise, which makes them more vulnerable to outside pressures – and that can lead to corruption.

'Today's gangsters need access to police computers on a regular basis and that means having a tame computer geek on the payroll,' explained one London detective.

Having access can help a criminal find out inside information about investigations, track down the addresses of officers and criminals and check for many other relevant flags, which might influence their criminal enterprises.

But it's hard to pinpoint who the crooked cops are when

it comes to computer staff because these specialised officers are usually highly skilled in covering their cyber tracks. Ultra-secure login facilities are supposed to help police guard against this type of corruption. But senior detectives believe that many computer cops already know their way around such security measures.

'A lot of the time, we don't necessarily even realise the police computer system has been compromised,' admitted one detective.

In other words, corrupt officers can work undetected for months at a time and often it's only sheer luck that helps others stumble on what they've been up to.

One recent example of this type of police corruption only came to light when an IT expert police officer was discovered at the home of a notorious cocaine baron during a raid. It turned out he was picking up a supply of drugs for himself as part of his 'payment' for helping the gangster.

One of the detectives involved in the case later told me: 'If we hadn't found him at that criminal's house, we'd never have known he was supplying information from the police database. The most disturbing aspect of this is that it must mean the majority of crooked computer cops remain undetected.'

EAVESDROPPING

Line of Duty makes electronic surveillance look very simple, but in the real world, it can be a very hit-and-miss way to gather evidence, especially when investigating corrupt officers.

One former detective explained: 'I've worked on many such

operations that ended in disaster because our listening devices didn't work properly or there were outside noises drowning out the voices of those we were listening to.'

The same detective added: 'I was on one investigation where we'd wired up a corrupt copper who'd agreed to help us nail two criminals who thought he was working for them. But this bent cop suddenly bottled it and flushed the bug down the toilet. We had no other back-up way to listen and abandoned the operation.

'It later emerged that the corrupt cop in question had been uncovered by the criminals and he was beaten to a pulp and nearly lost his life.'

He went on: 'Putting wires on people is so risky and I'd say that five out of ten of them are sussed out by the criminals and that can lead to really nasty reprisals.'

No wonder real-life police corruption revolves around a myriad of complex issues, which are often more far-reaching than anything portrayed on the small scene.

And what about the immense pressures that can so often cause a corrupt police officer to crack up?

DAMAGED

A few years ago, I was lucky enough to be given access for a television documentary to the inside of a convalescent home for police officers from across the UK. They were suffering psychological problems arising from incidents connected to their job. Amongst them were a number of corrupt officers, who'd literally cracked up. The police service were showing their caring side by being prepared to try and tackle such issues in an uncharacteristically open manner.

My visits to that specialised nursing home in the Home Counties enabled me to go inside the heads of corrupt officers to examine what makes them turn bad. One therapist – who'd treated numerous corrupt police officers – explained to me: 'Individuals react completely differently to the same problems and nowhere is this more apparent than in the police.

'Most officers are afraid to admit their problems to anyone inside their job environment for fear it might lead to their demotion or sometimes even dismissal. This puts up a barrier between individual officers, even if they're seemingly close friends.

'Some officers don't even tell their own wives or partners about their problems because they often see themselves as not being "allowed" to have any such issues because they deal with so many damaged people out on the streets.'

But experts say this simply puts additional pressure on police officers and forces them to hide their feelings even more. And – as we now know – that is very bad for mental health.

This particular therapist reckoned that at least 50 per cent of all corrupt police officers would not have ended up taking bribes if they'd had treatment to help them open up about personal problems: 'By repressing their true feelings, many police officers have developed mental problems, which undoubtedly affected their judgement when it comes to their work.'

This can be very damaging for the police and public at

large as it can also lead to false arrests and even unnecessary loss of life.

Another therapist said she tried to convince corrupt officers to admit their offences without fear of their lives being completely destroyed.

'That is the biggest barrier,' she explained. 'I want them to stop feeling guilt-ridden and needing to keep secrets. That in itself can help them turn over a new leaf in terms of their mental health.'

In *Line of Duty*, fleeting references are made to psychological evaluations and therapy, but some critics of the series from the real police say that storylines should hinge more on such emotive subjects.

One serving detective told me: 'For many generations this sort of stuff has been swept under the carpet. I believe the makers of *Line of Duty* have a duty to be even more transparent about mental-health issues because it could genuinely help cut down police corruption in the long term.'

One professional criminal I know told me recently that he had to seek out the help of a therapist to come to terms with his crimes and it is the same with corrupt police officers. 'I've dealt with a number of bent coppers and they always seem incredibly on edge. In many ways corrupt police officers need more help than anyone else.'

The same criminal continued: 'I've only just started to understand the demons in my early life that led me to join a crime family. It's the same with a corrupt cop. He may need to reach right back into his childhood to start to get some answers.

'I didn't trust anyone after what I went through as a kid and I thought that certain criminals were my saviours. It's the same with corrupt cops. They get disillusioned with the police for some reason or other and seek out the support of criminals, who can pay them enough money to get their lives back on track.'

But there are some officers who insist that the real-life equivalent of *Line of Duty*'s AC-12 should not employ officers with any mental-health issues.

ON THE EDGE

Line of Duty's AC-12 chief Ted Hastings' willingness to have 'fucked up' investigators on his team because he feels they'll be better suited to investigate corrupt cops is 'dangerous', according to some serving officers.

One recently retired detective explained: 'The personal problems of all the main characters who work inside AC-12 are very troubling. There is no way that those sorts of characters would end up in a police anti-corruption squad. They would be seen as a liability.'

In series one of *Line of Duty*, Steve Arnott guns down an innocent man during a police raid and this sends him crashing into depression and self-doubt until Ted Hastings comes along and 'rescues' him by offering him a new career challenge inside AC-12.

'Arnott was in deep shit,' one recently retired detective commented. 'He'd shot an innocent man dead and then along came Hastings like the Grim Reaper to offer Arnott a way out of his troubles. It just doesn't wash as far as most real officers are concerned. Arnott is a liability.'

This storyline particularly irritated some real police officers because it blatantly highlighted the implication that officers inside anti-corruption units were so flawed and vulnerable themselves that they could unfairly hurt their colleagues, even if they're innocent of corrupt practices.

The same recently retired officer explained: '*Line of Duty* has made us question the recruitment policy for anti-corruption units. Is it really healthy to use such flawed officers in the first place? Surely they'll be more trigger-happy because of what has happened to them in the past?'

No doubt the producers and writers of *Line of Duty* will insist that these characters are an accurate reflection of what they have been told by their police advisors. 'But just because their advisors have said something is accurate doesn't make it right, does it?' said one serving officer.

Yet some recently retired officers as well as production staff on *Line of Duty* insist the screwed-up backgrounds of characters like Arnott, Fleming and Hastings actually helps improve their skills to expose corrupt police officers.

The detective added: 'A lot of police officers think they're above the sort of domestic issues facing the lead characters in *Line of Duty* but everyone has, to a certain degree, problems of this nature.

'I believe the main characters on the show are better officers because they're able to empathise more with the corrupt officers and criminals they have to investigate. Surely that is the key to being an anti-corruption investigator, or a good copper for that matter?'

Another former officer put it like this: 'I think it's very smart of the writers and producers of *Line of Duty* to inject these sorts of problems into the characters. It makes us the audience relate much more closely to them and it helps us to understand the way they respond to specific situations.'

Some serving officers also believe that the level of openness in *Line of Duty* will give a lot of real-life coppers the courage to admit to their superiors when their lives are melting down, which could help prevent the temptation to take bribes.

One police officer explained: 'Coppers don't like telling their bosses about problems at home but *Line of Duty* shows you that there is nothing to be ashamed of. Everyone has problems.'

But some secrets can lead to monumental decisions.

SECRET LIVES

Up until less than twenty years ago there remained one outstanding highly emotive issue inside the UK's police forces, that of sexual orientation.

While *Line of Duty* hasn't starred any main characters who are gay, it seems only a matter of time before they're featured in the plotlines and many will no doubt say: 'About time too.'

But back in the 1980s and 1990s when AC-12's Arnott and Fleming were still toddlers, an officer's sexuality was still considered a serious security risk. Many officers rumoured to be gay were bullied and humiliated to such an extent that they were pushed out of the force before they'd even had a chance to defend themselves, let alone come out.

As one openly gay officer explained to me recently: 'Back then, gay people were ridiculed by the police. And the structure and management of the force meant that a person's sexuality was seen as something which could make them open to corruption.'

But of course this would never have been the case if officers in those days had been encouraged to be more open about their lifestyle choices in the first place.

Twenty years ago, I interviewed an old-school detective we'll call Lou, who admitted keeping his sexuality a secret from his colleagues, until a criminal tried to blackmail him into turning corrupt.

Lou explained: 'Most of my colleagues were extremely awkward around me because I wasn't married with children and I had a very soft voice, so I fitted into all their favourite stereotypes of a gay man. But I was extremely careful not to allow my lifestyle choices to overlap into any aspect of my job and for many years, I just got on with being a good, honest copper.'

But all this came crashing down for Lou when he arrested a member of one of the most notorious crime families in the Home Counties.

Lou explained: 'This gangster was furious he'd been nicked because he had a number of corrupt police officers on his payroll and expected them to get the charges against him dropped.'

Unknown to Lou, one of the gang's corrupt coppers told

his criminal paymasters that Lou was gay and they put a shadow on him. This soon led to Lou being sent photos of himself in a street holding hands with another man in the West End of London.

Lou recalled: 'Soon after I saw the photos, I was approached by one of the henchmen from this gang, who tried to force me to accept a bribe. I told him to get lost and reported everything to my senior officer.'

But Lou's boss was very unhelpful and Lou was convinced he'd soon be pushed out of the force for admitting to being gay. 'It felt like I had no support from above,' he explained. 'My boss didn't seem sympathetic and even accused me of exposing myself to blackmail by being gay. He said he'd sent a file on my case up to his superiors and was awaiting a decision.

'It was a horrible time and I seriously considered suicide because I was so fearful about what would happen once my gay lifestyle was exposed to all my colleagues.'

After a few days, Lou demanded an update from his boss. 'He was really dismissive and said it could be months before I'd know if I would face any disciplinary action.'

A few days later, Lou visited his force's anti-corruption unit.

'It was a massive step to take and I was very nervous,' he explained. 'But a woman officer in the unit was extremely sympathetic and she persuaded me to turn the whole thing on its head.'

Lou ended up secretly recording the henchman and his boss trying to blackmail him into taking bribes. They were arrested and Lou decided to come out to all his colleagues. 'There were a lot of raised eyebrows about my sexuality at first but the success of the police operation to take down that crime family overrode all that in the end. It was such a relief not to have to pretend any more. I was able to be myself for the first time in my professional life.'

But Lou remains convinced that numerous other gay officers from those 'bad old days' would not have been so lucky.

He added: 'It's so sad that being a secretly gay officer back then made you so vulnerable to corruption. I remember a couple of other detectives where I worked also being compromised by their sexuality. Their senior officers offered no real support and tried to keep it secret from the outside world because they considered it "bad publicity" for the police.

Today those attitudes no longer exist and the diverse sexuality of officers is now considered a strength, not a weakness. About time too!

'I love *Line of Duty* but I do sometimes wonder how Ted Hastings would deal with a problem with a gay officer because he does seem a bit old school.'

THE RACE CARD

'Don't talk to me about victimisation... nobody's blacker than me, son.'

Line of Duty's corrupt DCI Tony Gates to Steve Arnott in series one.

The series has tried its hardest to accurately reflect many

aspects of modern-day policing but the jury's still out on the issue of race on the show's five series to date. Amongst the UK's real police there is little doubt that racism still exists in The Job to this day. As a result, many officers in today's police forces across the UK are concerned about how *Line of Duty* is reflecting this highly sensitive issue.

One officer explained: 'Series one featured a suspected corrupt black officer but there was no indication of racism towards him. There was a similar situation in a later series when a young black detective joined AC-12.'

To be fair to the makers of *Line of Duty*, the entire issue of race is a tricky tightrope to walk.

Another serving officer explained: 'I think the programme's makers handled it with great subtlety. Why should it be turned into an issue? Surely it's much better to ignore it and treat every character on his or her own merits? That is exactly what they've done.'

But black officers I've spoken to in recent years insist that the problem of racism is far from over in the real police. 'I can assure you there is still underlying racism when it comes to non-white officers,' one told me.

'When I first joined the police almost twenty years ago, I was made to feel particularly unwelcome. Back then, there was still a stereotypical response to black people by most officers, who believed we were more likely to be involved in criminal activities than white people.'

But there have also been a few real-life officers of colour who've been suspected of using their race as an excuse for corrupt practices.

Fifteen years ago, Ali Dizaei was Britain's highest-ranking Asian police officer. He was even presented with the Long Service and Good Conduct Medal by then Scotland Yard Commissioner, Sir Ian Blair.

Then in September 2008, Dizaei was suspended from his police job on full pay amid claims that he was corrupt.

On 8 February 2010, he was convicted on charges of perverting the course of justice and of misconduct in a public office. Dizaei – jailed for four years – was the most senior policeman in more than thirty years to be given a prison sentence. A few weeks later, he was formally dismissed from the Metropolitan Police.

Then, on 16 May 2011, Dizaei's appeal against his conviction was quashed and he was released from prison. However, after a retrial the following year, he was again found guilty of the same charges. This time he was sentenced to three years' imprisonment.

Dizaei appealed again but that appeal was dismissed on 14 February 2013. The Lord Chief Justice said that 'the guilty verdict was fully justified' and that the conviction 'was and remains safe'.

It was a spectacular fall from grace for a police commander who'd once been in charge of 5,000 officers across the west of London.

A few years ago, I tracked Ali Dizaei down and persuaded him to meet me on his old manor of west London. His insight into the world of corrupt policing was an eye-opener and he insisted that he'd been 'framed' by corrupt racist officers afraid he would spill the beans on them.

Dizaei's main purpose in meeting me was to discuss a new book he planned to write giving his own account of his career. As he explained all this to me, it was hard to work out whether his take on corruption was simply a smokescreen for his own involvement. Or maybe he'd genuinely been caught up in the middle of something so toxic it cost him his career? He also peppered the conversation with references to the racist attitudes of some of his colleagues.

But what happens when a real-life racist murder is covered up by the most corrupt police officers in UK criminal history?

Chapter Six

MY REAL LINE OF DUTY

'You need to watch yer step. We know where your kids go to school.'

Phone threat made to me in 1997

STEPHEN LAWRENCE RIP

It would be remiss not to include one of the most notorious and tragic cases of police corruption in recent years, and that is the murder of Stephen Lawrence.

On a mild spring night on 22 April 1993 in Well Hall, Eltham, south-east London, teenager Stephen Lawrence – from nearby Plumstead – was viciously stabbed to death. It was an unprovoked attack by a gang of white youths while he waited with his friend Duwayne Brooks at a bus stop.

Over the days that followed, police received several tip-offs naming the most likely suspects as brothers Neil and Jamie Acourt, Gary Dobson, and David Norris. Three days later, officers even took a statement from the alleged victim of another stabbing committed by the same suspects.

However – despite seeming to already have enough evidence to make arrests – police instead launched a surveillance operation on the four suspects' homes. At one stage officers saw them walking out of a house carrying bin bags and driving away. But the police investigators did not follow them because – they later claimed – they didn't have a mobile phone with which to call their commanding officer for his orders.

One of the suspects, David Norris, was the son of a local criminal, Clifford Norris, who would eventually be alleged to have had corrupt relationships with south London police officers. Clifford Norris's family members later claimed he used a network of corrupt Metropolitan Police officers to protect himself, his criminal associates and his close relations from justice.

Most detectives involved in the Stephen Lawrence murder inquiry didn't realise that Norris's south London crime boss was already pulling the strings from his nearby prison cell. This villain had initially been infuriated to find himself dragged into a murder inquiry. He was trying to quietly serve out the remaining months of his sentence for his involvement with one of the biggest armed robberies of the 1980s and needed to keep a low profile in order to qualify for parole.

But this same crime boss knew full well that his connections to detectives in south-east London were a potential source of power and influence. He believed that if he could help get a murder investigation shelved then it would be something he could always hold over any corrupt officers on his payroll.

Two south London underworld sources told me that this same crime boss asked his Scotland Yard handlers to help ensure Clifford Norris's son David and his co-suspects would not be charged with murder following the killing of Stephen Lawrence.

Unknown to the Lawrence family, police officers had also launched an unofficial surveillance operation targeting Stephen's parents, Doreen and Neville Lawrence, in the days following the murder. Their plan was to dig up some dirt, which could then be used to persuade their bosses to pull back on the murder inquiry.

'*Line of Duty* looks like child's play compared to what was happening after the murder of Stephen Lawrence,' one former south London detective later told me. 'This was a blatant attempt at perverting the course of justice and it was clear certain corrupt officers would stop at nothing to make sure Stephen's death was not properly investigated.'

Behind the scenes of this real-life police corruption scandal loomed an imposing, power-crazy senior police officer not dissimilar from John Corbett in series five of *Line of Duty* combined with crooked cop Tony Gates from series one of the show.

Back on the real mean streets of south-east London, this senior officer had long been rumoured to be 'much too close' to certain high-powered criminals in the Home Counties at that time.

One recently retired London detective later told me: 'This bloke was a copper's copper. He got big results but we all wondered about him as a character for many years. He seemed flawed, but no one had the bottle to confront him because we all knew he'd probably win any challenge.'

This senior officer, he said, was playing a waiting game when it came to the Stephen Lawrence murder inquiry. He believed that with the right approaches to certain detectives involved in the Lawrence case, he'd be able to 'sort it all out' and make sure that his prime informants from the underworld would be kept happy.

'He was sharp, smart and had a lot of bottle. Many of us looked up to him, despite all his flaws. And he was so approachable, so relaxed, that a lot of us fell under his spell,' added the same retired detective.

It was later disclosed that at one stage, Duwayne Brooks – sole witness to Stephen Lawrence's murder – was even guarded by police officers alleged to have corrupt links to Clifford Norris and his crime boss.

But there was a lot worse than that to come.

COVER-UP CONTINUES

Ten days after the murder of Stephen Lawrence, the teenager's grieving parents held a press conference to talk about their frustrations that not enough was being done to catch the killers. The murder investigation was already sparking controversy because police had made no actual arrests, despite being given the names of the suspects.

Two days later, Doreen and Neville Lawrence met Nelson Mandela when he made a high-profile visit to London. They hoped that the accompanying publicity might put more pressure on Scotland Yard to step up their investigation into the murder of Stephen.

But unknown to his parents and the general public, police officers continued secretly spying on Mr and Mrs Lawrence. It's alleged that certain officers still believed they could get the investigation to switch directions if they were able to prove Stephen's family had criminal connections. Nothing could have been further from the truth and after weeks of secret surveillance, this underground police operation against the family finally fizzled out.

However, the publicity surrounding Mr and Mrs Lawrence's meeting with Nelson Mandela did manage to put the police under enough pressure for them to reluctantly insist the arrests of the chief suspects remained their priority.

Between 7 May and 23 June 1993, the Acourt brothers, Dobson, Norris, and another suspect, Luke Knight, were detained by murder-squad detectives. Witness Duwayne Brooks identified Acourt and Knight from an ID parade as being involved in the killing of his friend, Stephen Lawrence. The pair were charged with murder. They denied all the allegations.

But at least one high-ranking officer was continuing to influence the investigation. In July 1993, charges against Acourt and Knight were dropped, following a meeting between the Crown Prosecution Service (CPS) and the police.

The CPS insisted the evidence provided by sole witness Brooks had been unreliable, after one officer made a statement claiming Brooks had admitted to him he was 'unsure' about the men he'd picked out at that identity parade. Brooks later denied saying this.

The Stephen Lawrence case was unfolding with the same sort of dramatic 'beats' as a *Line of Duty* plotline complete with a murder victim, allegedly corrupt and racist police and professional criminals lurking in the background.

Then in December 1993, Southwark coroner Sir Montague Levine halted an inquest into Stephen Lawrence's death after the family's barrister, Michael Mansfield QC, told the court there was 'dramatic' new evidence, including information positively identifying three of the original suspects.

However, the CPS later stated the new evidence was insufficient to support murder charges, and the case against the men was dropped yet again. Details of this new evidence have never been revealed publicly.

In September 1994, disillusioned parents Neville and Doreen launched their own private prosecution against suspects Acourt, Knight and Dobson. This was to be a standard criminal trial, although not brought by the CPS.

A few weeks later, a second police investigation was opened under the management of two senior Metropolitan Police officers.

In December 1994, a secret video camera was hidden in suspect Dobson's flat. Footage and accompanying audio clearly showed him and Norris making obscene racist remarks. Acourt and Knight were also filmed using violent and racist language, but none of this was considered as sufficient evidence to prosecute the suspects.

The Lawrence case then disappeared from the public eye until April 1996, when the family's private prosecution of Acourt, Knight and Dobson at the Old Bailey collapsed. Mr

Justice Curtis ruled that identification evidence from Brooks remained inadmissible. The three men were acquitted and they could not be tried again because they'd been found not guilty.

In the badlands of south-east London, the aforementioned crime boss and other professional criminals believed their tame corrupt police officers had done enough to stop the Stephen Lawrence murder inquiry in its tracks.

To make matters worse, the then Conservative Home Secretary Michael Howard refused to see the Lawrences to discuss the case. This further fuelled allegations of racism and a cover-up.

It seemed as if corrupt police officers had won their duplicitous battle to get the murder inquiry shelved before it had even been properly dealt with in a court of law.

One hard-working and honest retired south London detective later told me: 'It was sickening. Certain officers were so clearly happy the case appeared to have been dropped. They were saying it was just a black kid who was murdered and no one cared about it. They were still ranting on about protecting their underworld sources being much more important for the police in general.

'But some of us were convinced that crime boss and other professional criminals had a hold over certain officers. This meant they'd been obliged to try and ambush the murder inquiry. We thought maybe that crime boss was blackmailing some officers because his power and influence over them seemed extraordinary.'

But it didn't end there he said: 'Honest cops like me were

sneered at by those corrupt officers and their friends. They accused us of being "troublemakers" and claimed they needed to keep their criminal informants happy in order to get others banged up.'

Others were claiming that the race-hate aspects of the killing also had an influence on the decision not to continue the murder investigation.

'MURDERERS' EXPOSED

In February 1997, there was yet another twist in the extraordinary story of bringing to justice the murderers of Stephen Lawrence. A coroner's inquest ended with a verdict of 'unlawful killing in a completely unprovoked racist attack by five youths'.

The Lawrence family immediately complained formally to the Police Complaints Authority (PCA) about the police's handling of the investigation. A few days later, the *Daily Mail* published the names and photographs of the two Acourt brothers, Norris, Knight, and Dobson under the headline: 'Murderers'. The paper accused the men of killing Stephen Lawrence and challenged them to sue for libel.

In July 1997, new Labour Home Secretary Jack Straw met Stephen Lawrence's parents. The Home Office then announced a judicial inquiry into the case to be led by retired high court judge, Sir William Macpherson. At last, the Lawrences' fight for justice seemed to be gaining ground.

PROBING THE TRUTH

As a result of my inside knowledge of the south-east London underworld and its connections to the Lawrence case, I was hired in 1997 to work as an investigator on the Macpherson inquiry.

Up until now, I've avoided publicly mentioning my own direct involvement in something I wouldn't normally want to reveal as it would be seen by many as stepping across journalistic boundaries. But this specific police corruption case is so far-reaching that I feel obliged to come clean about my involvement.

My role in all of this came about through the police, lawyers and criminals I've interviewed for my true-crime books about some of Britain's most notorious professional criminals over the past twenty-five years.

During those inquiries, I discovered that the father of one of the main suspects in the murder of Stephen Lawrence was a criminal associate of a notorious gang boss, who told his police handlers that he'd refuse to help their inquiries into other crimes unless investigating officers watered down their hunt for the killers.

Those same officers allegedly decided to help their criminal informants because they were considered more important than a dead black teenager.

QC Mike Mansfield and the Lawrences' solicitor Imran Khan asked me to find out about alleged police corruption behind how and why the suspects were released.

In December 1997, a PCA report on the original

investigation of Stephen Lawrence's murder highlighted 'significant weaknesses, omissions and lost opportunities'. The question of police corruption had by this time disappeared from the agenda, no doubt to the relief of many officers in south London. The focus was now on race issues, even though the PCA insisted there was no evidence of racist conduct by police.

As one former south London detective from that era later explained: 'Back then, being racist was a much easier pill to swallow than corruption for the police. It's ironic, isn't it? But it seemed to many of us that while racism was definitely an issue in the Lawrence case, it was not as significant as corruption.'

THREATS

Within weeks of being employed by the Macpherson inquiry team to dig further into the corruption allegations I got my first taste of what was to come. A man's voice on my home phone said simply: 'We know where your kids go to school.'

It seemed that certain corrupt police officers and their criminal associates would stop at nothing to prevent me from trying to uncover the truth about their involvement in the Lawrence case.

I received more death threats over the following weeks and eventually I was advised to withdraw from the Macpherson inquiry team because of fears over my safety and that of my family.

Detectives and lawyers working on the inquiry persuaded me to go back one last time to an important criminal source for further evidence of police corruption in the Lawrence case. But when I tried to contact him, I discovered he'd disappeared.

It felt as if I'd pushed my luck as far as I could.

As one former south London detective later told me: 'Bent coppers are much more dangerous than your usual everyday villains. They're trapped in a cycle of shame. They know if anyone exposes them, then it will be the end of their profession. That's quite a lot of pressure to be under.'

Also, completely unknown to me, a group of renegade corrupt police officers who worked for the *News of the World* tabloid newspaper had hacked my phone in a bid to try and find out who my sources were re the police corruption connections to the Stephen Lawrence case.

In June 1998, the five individuals alleged to have murdered Stephen Lawrence gave evidence at the public inquiry overseen by Lord Macpherson, having been told they would face prosecution if they did not appear.

Outside the inquiry building, police had to fire CS gas at protesters as the suspects arrived. Members of the Nation of Islam group even stormed the building and branded the inquiry a sham. As a result, the case had to be adjourned for three hours.

The following month, Metropolitan Police anti-corruption investigators were given the name of an officer who served on the first Lawrence murder investigation, by one of his colleagues. They were told this officer's corrupt links to criminals in south-east England may have influenced the murder probe by police.

Just as so often occurs in *Line of Duty*, the 'outing' of one officer as corrupt by a colleague provoked a fierce backlash against that informant.

One former south London detective explained: 'I was told the officer who gave the name of the bent copper connected to the Lawrence case was spat on and had his locker smashed up. There was a lot of anger against him for daring to taint the reputation of a fellow officer.'

It was also rumoured that the same police officer informant had earlier been arrested for his role inside a corrupt unit of south London officers and had 'grassed up' a colleague to secure immunity from prosecution.

Stephen Lawrence's parents then called on the then Metropolitan Police Commissioner Sir Paul Condon to resign for police failings. He refused but did make an unprecedented apology to them, saying: 'I'm truly sorry that we let you down.' But he made no direct reference to the role of police corruption in the Stephen Lawrence murder case.

Why was Scotland Yard running scared?

WHITEWASH

In February 1999, the Macpherson Report came out and found the police guilty of mistakes and 'institutional racism', and made seventy recommendations on changes to policing and wider public policy. It advised strengthening the Race Relations Act to tackle discrimination. The report also suggested a rethink of the principle of 'double jeopardy', to allow the retrial of acquitted defendants in exceptional circumstances if new evidence emerged of their guilt.

Buried inside the report were just a couple of sentences vaguely referring to how the Lawrence case might have been influenced by police corruption.

Despite providing my own detailed evidence backing up these claims, as well as likely numerous others, they were reduced to just a few lines.

Only one officer was criticised in the Macpherson Report for his handling of potentially significant witnesses during the Lawrence investigation. But the inquiry subsequently cleared him of any corrupt motive. Yet this same much-heralded report was hailed by UK politicians and lawmakers as 'one of the most important moments in the modern history of criminal justice in Britain'.

Many detectives thought otherwise.

'What a load of old tosh!' said one retired south London officer. 'We had a right laugh at that. In a nutshell, bent coppers had managed to pull the wool over the eyes of all the pen-pushing office-bound bosses, who were desperate not to rock any boats.

'It looked like all the senior officers were so desperate to kick all the corruption stuff off the agenda that they took the racism accusations on the chin.'

In April 1999, all five primary suspects in the murder of Stephen Lawrence denied involvement in the murder in a TV interview with broadcast journalist Martin Bashir. After it was aired, they accused the programme's makers, Granada Television, of editing the footage to make them look guilty.

But the Lawrence case was about to swerve in a completely different direction.

THE 'PAY-OFF'

In December 2000, the Metropolitan Police paid the Lawrence family £320,000 in damages. Some inside the police tried to sneeringly imply this was some kind of 'hush money' for the family. But nothing could have been further from the truth because the Lawrences were determined to continue their fight for justice.

As one retired south London detective later explained: 'The big bosses at the yard had bottled it completely. They thought they could bung a few bob at the family and it would all finally go away. Then they could sweep all that talk of police corruption under the carpet for ever.'

But Mr and Mrs Lawrence were not going to be silenced that easily. Behind the scenes they continued their battle for justice, although to many it seemed like an uphill task.

Then in April 2002, a former detective who served on the original Lawrence murder inquiry alleged that one of his fellow officers had corrupt links to criminal Clifford Norris, father of suspect David Norris. But this was only briefly reported in the mainstream media.

In September 2002, suspects David Norris and Neil Acourt were jailed for eighteen months for a racist attack on an off-duty black policeman the previous year. The court heard that Norris threw a drink and shouted racist abuse from a car driven by Acourt.

Then the Lawrence story once again went stony silent. Had the corrupt cops won the day after all? There is no doubt they certainly thought so.

'They were implying they'd finally killed it off,' one retired south London detective recalled. 'Their arrogance seemed to know no bounds. They were covering their backs and no doubt keeping their criminal friends safe.'

In April 2005, the UK's double jeopardy legal principle – which had prevented suspects from being tried twice for the same crime – was scrapped for certain offences if there was sufficient new evidence.

Many expected an immediate response from the Crown Prosecution Service re the Lawrence case but instead there was yet another deathly silence.

Then in July 2006, a BBC documentary alleged that suspect David Norris's criminal father Clifford paid an officer who worked on the murder inquiry in order to be kept one step ahead of the investigation. The then Independent Police Complaints Commission (IPCC) investigated the claims but insisted there was no police corruption or dishonest links between Clifford Norris and the officer in question.

'It wouldn't have been believable if it had been part of the plot of an episode of *Line of Duty*,' one former south London detective explained. 'It felt to most coppers that the emphasis had always been on protecting the reputation of Scotland Yard at all costs. The attitude was still that it was better for the police to simply ignore all these corruption issues.'

But other lawmakers outside the police were determined to plough on, although it would take another five years to achieve a breakthrough.

In May 2011, the UK's court of appeal agreed to quash

Dobson's 1996 acquittal for the murder of Stephen Lawrence in the face of new forensic evidence.

It emerged that the victim's DNA had been found on a blood spot on Dobson's jacket – with a one-in-a-billion chance of the blood coming from anyone other than Stephen. There were also two hairs belonging to Stephen found in an evidence bag recovered from Norris's bedroom.

And evidence of a conspiracy by corrupt police officers continued to be downplayed, even though it was clearly dogging the case.

HACKED

In the summer of 2011, an ex-detective I knew informed me that one of the retired police officers hacking phones on behalf of the *News of the World* had close ties to some of the police officers suspected of corruption following the Stephen Lawrence murder.

In my case, it appeared that certain corrupt officers had been trying to find out who my sources were. A few months later, Rupert Murdoch, the owner of the *News of the World*, paid out many millions of pounds in compensation to so-called hacking victims, including myself. But no one ever specifically apologised for the actions of that former police officer.

In November 2011, Dobson and Norris's murder trial began at the Old Bailey. Mr Justice Treacy told the jury they should disregard previous publicity and 'start this case with a clean slate'. Covert police surveillance video evidence from the 1990s was shown in the court. It featured Norris talking about 'skinning' black people and setting them alight.

In January 2012, Dobson and Norris were found guilty of murder, eighteen years after Stephen Lawrence was killed in cold blood. Both men received life sentences. In a statement read out by his solicitors, Stephen's father Neville said he was 'full of joy and relief' at the conviction.

And then the rumours of police corruption resurfaced once again.

In June 2013, UK media outlets alleged that former Metropolitan Police officer-turned-whistle-blower Peter Francis was one of the officers sent to spy on the Lawrence family to 'dig up dirt' on them in the period shortly after the murder in April 1993. It was also alleged that senior officers deliberately withheld that information from the Macpherson inquiry.

The Stephen Lawrence case refused to die.

EXPOSED

In the spring of 2014, a review of police corruption claims was ordered by the then Home Secretary, Theresa May, after reports in the media – including an article I wrote for the *Mail on Sunday* on 14 March – about police corruption connections to the murder of Stephen Lawrence.

A major review of the case by Mark Ellison QC then confirmed new allegations that the Metropolitan Police had another spy working within the 'Lawrence family camp' during the course of the judicial inquiry into matters arising from his death.

Then, the Independent Police Complaints Commission found that a former senior officer – who'd met an undercover officer in 1998 during the Macpherson inquiry – should have faced disciplinary proceedings. This was the same officer who'd allegedly 'obtained information pertaining to the Lawrence family and their supporters, potentially undermining the inquiry and public confidence'.

As had so often been the case when it comes to police corruption, the officer in question had been hurriedly retired in order to avoid any embarrassing revelations coming out.

In the middle of 2016, Lawrence murder suspect Jaimie Acourt's connections to the south London underworld were further confirmed when he abandoned his partner and two children to go on the run to Spain, after being linked to a drugs gang.

Around this time, I received an email from a prison officer who worked at the jail where Clifford Norris's notorious crime boss was now incarcerated. He'd scribbled a threat against me at the start of a book I'd written.

The page in that book now takes pride of place in a picture frame on my office wall.

It reads:

> *Wensley Clarkson has printed loads of lies about me in his books and caused untold damage. The tables will turn one day.*

So the threats against me kept coming. It seems that many police officers and criminals had a lot to lose unless the Stephen Lawrence case 'went away'.

THE C-WORD

In April 2018, Scotland Yard Commissioner Cressida Dick claimed Scotland Yard had been 'transformed' in the two decades since it had been branded institutionally racist in the 1999 Macpherson Report.

Commissioner Dick later insisted she 'did not recognise' claims that the Metropolitan Police was still institutionally racist and said the term was 'not helpful or accurate'. Once again, racism NOT corruption was being talked about by Scotland Yard's propaganda machine.

The Commissioner also insisted all recommendations for police in the Macpherson Report had been fulfilled. But Stephen Lawrence's mother Doreen insisted the fight against police racism had 'stagnated'.

A few weeks later, Lawrence suspect and fugitive Jamie Acourt was caught leaving a gym in Barcelona, Spain, and extradited back to the UK to face allegations that he ran a drug gang.

Meanwhile, the National Crime Agency were quietly working away on Operation Probitas, which had been launched on behalf of the police watchdog, the Independent Office for Police Conduct. It was allegedly going to concentrate exclusively on police corruption issues relating to the Lawrence case. But few believed it would do so. The investigation's prime target was said to be the same detective who'd been earlier told no evidence of corruption had been found against him.

Stephen Lawrence's best friend and witness to his murder, Duwayne Brooks, said this latest investigation was unlikely to uncover anything new. And he said of the NCA inquiry: 'It's a slap in the face to myself and the Lawrence family and everyone who has suffered from police corruption.'

Others called it a prime example of the police 'going through the motions' because they wanted to finally kill the corruption rumours stone dead.

Then in the early summer of 2018, two detectives from the National Crime Agency involved in the latest inquiry into police corruption during the Lawrence murder investigation decided to widen their inquiries. These officers were from Northern Ireland's police force and were considered more impartial than UK mainland police officers.

But were the police just trying to silence their critics once and for all?

NAILED

One source recently told me that certain members of the Freemasons closed rank to protect the same crime boss (who was a member) as well as his sidekick, Clifford Norris (father of Lawrence suspect and also allegedly a Freemason). It was even alleged to me that certain Freemasons put pressure on one corrupt officer to drop the Lawrence inquiry after some senior officers labelled it an 'insignificant crime', which of course was the original point behind the Stephen Lawrence 'cover-up'.

But even more extraordinary was the admission by NCA investigator Alan Dornan that his inquiry did not even have the legal power to use information gathered on behalf of the Macpherson Report as relevant evidence in a court of law.

Clearly, London's Metropolitan Police remained obsessed with clearing their name when it came to corruption allegations linked to the aftermath of the Lawrence murder. Was this the reason behind the police's decision to ignore Doreen Lawrence's plea to end all inquiries connected to her son's murder?

There have been a number of examples on *Line of Duty* of crooked officers who've deliberately tried to get criminals off charges. But nothing on the scale that was still being alleged to have happened with the Lawrence case.

As one recently retired detective added: 'Those crooked cops could never have envisaged the way that the Lawrence case turned into a national scandal. They'd looked on it as nothing more than the street murder of a black man. Such crimes were not a priority back then.'

I'd been interviewed twice at the National Crime Agency headquarters because of my knowledge of police corruption involving officers connected to the Lawrence case. Yet the new information I provided has not – at the time of writing – led to any further developments with regard to corrupt police involvement in the case.

I'd personally been threatened and my home had even been broken into, with my laptops and notes being stolen without a trace.

I've even been told by one retired officer that 'it is highly likely' that my original submission to the Macpherson inquiry was removed from the Macpherson 'file' before the information in it was even seen by Lord Macpherson and his team.

It was clear from my meetings with the NCA that they

did not interview most of the important potential witnesses/suspects. This included the senior crooked policemen who made a call to the police station handling Stephen's murder investigation on behalf of that crime boss.

I've tried on numerous occasions to speak to the senior police officer who many believe was behind the lenient treatment of the Lawrence murder suspects. None of his associates will talk to me, either. I did manage to leave a message on the landline at his holiday home in Western Europe some time ago but, surprise, surprise, he didn't return my call.

So what was the point of this latest investigation into police corruption connected to the murder of Stephen Lawrence?

IN CONCLUSION

The NCA probe was described to me by one retired detective as a waste of public money. 'Too little, too late,' he said. There have been no arrests and very few people even interviewed in connection with the main allegations. What was the point of it all?

It remains clear that a web of corrupt police officers did influence the Stephen Lawrence murder case for many years.

So, is this impasse between so-called bent coppers and Scotland Yard's top brass likely to continue?

No one seems prepared or able to answer that question.

LINE OF DUTY – WHAT NEXT?

Series six of *Line of Duty* is one of the most hotly anticipated drama shows in recent UK TV history. Rumours about new plotlines, murders and mayhem have flooded social media since the next series was announced at the end of 2019.

All three main AC-12 characters will of course be returning: Ted Hastings (Adrian Dunbar), Kate Fleming (Vicky McClure) and Steve Arnott (Martin Compston). The storyline will be set a year and a half on from the events of series five.

The first read-through of the script for the new series occurred in February 2020. BBC One's official Twitter page posted a picture of the AC-12 'gang of three' alongside brand new prime nemesis Detective Chief Inspector Joanne Davidson, played by Scottish actress Kelly Macdonald. This actress got her first big break in *Trainspotting* more than twenty-five years ago.

More recently, Kelly has starred in *The Victim* and *Girl/*

Haji – as well as being known for her roles in *Gosford Park*, *State of Play*, *No Country for Old Men* and *Boardwalk Empire*.

Actor Martin Compston was so impressed by Kelly Macdonald's credentials that he wrote gushingly on Twitter: 'Another magnificent addition to the *Line of Duty* team. Said it before, huge part of the show's success is the phenomenal guest actors we've had. Kelly Macdonald will be up there with the best of them, what a talent, what a career. Buzzing to get the tape started.'

Compston also shared a photo of himself in police uniform with co-star Adrian Dunbar and *Line of Duty* creator Jed Mercurio. However, Vicky McClure's absence from the photo sparked typically wild rumours that her character Kate Fleming might be the elusive 'H' whom AC-12 have been chasing throughout the whole series.

Also joining the three main characters in series six will be actors Shalom Brune-Franklin (*Our Girl*), Andi Osho (*Kiri*) and Prasanna Puwanarajah (*Doctor Foster*). Perry Fitzpatrick will also be part of the cast, having previously appeared opposite Vicky McClure in Channel 4's *This Is England* and *I Am Nicola*.

It was also rumoured that Taj Atwal (PC Tatleen Sohota) and Aiysha Hart (Murder Squad cop DS Sam Railston) would be making comebacks on series six following earlier appearances.

Actress Polly Walker's character Gill Biggeloe is still alive but has been given a new identity since seducing Ted Hastings in series three and then almost destroying his career in series five. But that doesn't necessarily rule out her character returning.

Creator Jed Mercurio and his *Line of Duty* production team were at the time of writing hopeful that the new series would be aired before the end of 2020. However, the coronavirus pandemic meant that only the first four episodes had completed filming by mid-March before the world went on an anti-virus lockdown.

Meanwhile, avid *Line of Duty* fans speculated that Mercurio had deliberately planted a number of clues about the series six plot in the previous series five. This of course had centred around rogue undercover officer John Corbett (Stephen Graham). He'd been apparently prepared go to any lengths to catch 'H', the crooked copper at the heart of the Organised Crime Group (OCG), who were the driving force behind much of the corruption being investigated by AC-12.

As series five progressed, we learned that Corbett had links to AC-12 chief Ted Hastings because his mother, Anne-Marie, had been a police informant who had a relationship – professional and perhaps more – with Hastings when he was a young RUC officer during The Troubles in Northern Ireland.

In series five, manipulative lawyer Gill Biggeloe – who was secretly in league with that OCG – deliberately gave Corbett the impression that Hastings had been responsible for Anne-Marie's death at the hands of paramilitary forces. As a result, Corbett became obsessed with proving Hastings was a bent copper. But his mission was cut short when the OCG discovered Corbett was a rat and slit his throat.

However, the big question from series five was how did

the OCG find out Corbett's true identity? By the end of that series, it still wasn't clear. According to OCG member Lisa McQueen, Corbett's cover had been blown following a tip-off from Lee Banks, an imprisoned henchman from the same gang.

In that case, where did Banks get this information from? Although never proven, many suspected Ted Hastings might have been the source.

But one fan pointed out: 'Scriptwriters like Jed Mercurio love taking an audience up a classic red herring path and then suddenly surprising everyone by coming from a completely different "direction".'

And of course in series five Hastings was let off the hook when it was discovered that he'd been framed by his onetime lover Biggeloe, who'd become obsessed with proving that Hastings was 'H'. Hastings remains clearly on thin ice after what happened to him towards the end of season five. Some avid *Line of Duty* fans have even pointed out that although Hastings returned to active duty at the end of that series, he was not completely off the hook when the closing credits came up on the very last episode.

There were also rumours on the TV grapevine that six could be the final series of *Line of Duty*. But few inside the television world believe this will be the case. One BBC producer said: 'The show is a gold mine for the corporation. Jed Mercurio has consistently written superb scripts and there is no reason why *Line of Duty* can't become the longest-running police drama in UK TV history.'

Adrian Dunbar was asked in the middle of 2019 if the

show was going to stretch beyond series six. He would only say: 'We'll have to wait and see. The standard of the writing is so high, you know. If Jed keeps doing it, we could go on for ever.'

Expect to also see more of Fleming and Arnott's personal lives as they struggle with the balance between love, family and work. Many fans are hoping they will rekindle the brief affair they had in series one.

In the midst of all this, another teaser for the upcoming series was planted in the heads of fans when Ted Hastings was pictured during the first few days of series six filming sporting a ring on his wedding finger, despite the fact he and his wife Roisin have long been estranged.

Roisin had been last seen in hospital in series five after being attacked by corrupt Scouser cop John Corbett. She told husband Ted to leave her alone after he suggested he would have protected her, had they still been living together.

And clearly, creator Jed Mecurio is unable to resist teasing fans on Twitter. He shared one photo from filming of series six which showed Kate Fleming and Steve Arnott pointing guns at one another. Next to them is a passed-out Ted Hastings slumped on a chair. A giant 'H' lies against him, implying that he is the infamous and criminal mastermind whose legion of bent coppers had infiltrated AC-12.

It's obviously a picture set up by Mercurio to blatantly tantilise fans of the show. On the other hand, he could be pulling off the ultimate double bluff.

Then Mercurio sparked even more speculation about the identity of bent copper H when he whipped up a social media storm by sharing a photo of Australian chocolate biscuits Tim Tams with the caption: #LineofDuty Series 6 Plot Clue No. 1

Manufactured by a company called Arnott's, the cryptic snap sent viewers into a frenzy, with theories ranging from a move to Australia by Steve to him breaking up with his girlfriend.

One whimsical viewer even wrote: 'Steve's going to leave the force and set up a biscuit company? My theory is that because the biscuit company is Arnott's and the biscuit bar is breaking, it must mean Steve will break up with his girlfriend and end up investigating her or someone else in his department.'

On 4 March 2020, Piers Morgan on GMTV's breakfast show asked Ted Hastings actor Adrian Dunbar: 'So who is H?'

Dunbar smiled and then changed the subject. But he did admit that there was a possibility that the coronavirus pandemic might be 'crowbarred' into the sixth series script because of its enormity.

Dunbar said: 'We have no idea what happens after the current four episodes. That helps our performance.'

And he insisted: 'Even I don't know if Hastings is straight or dishonest.'

THE LAST WORD

Video footage of corrupt officers secretly filmed taking bribes and commissioning hitmen to kill their colleagues not surprisingly makes compelling viewing for *Line of Duty*'s vast audience.

Watching senior officer John Corbett – played so brilliantly by Stephen Graham – strolling into a big-time drug deal in series five perfectly sums it all up. He has immense pressures at home and work and literally cracks up.

As one recently retired south London detective explained: 'Crooked cops are flagrantly defying society and giving the rest of us a bad name, so when they claim pressure caused this it is a weak excuse, to put it mildly.'

But psychiatrists often refer to what we're talking about here as 'underlying terror'. While it's clearly no excuse for double-dealing cops to inflict immense harm on everyone, it is worth explaining here. For many real-life corrupt cops walk a deadly line between crime and punishment. They often act as if they're masters of their own destiny, while in reality nothing could be further from the truth because they live in fear of being exposed.

'The underlying terror kicks in and they become virtually frozen,' explained one psychiatrist. 'That makes them unable to move in any tangible direction.'

As a result, the police officer perpetrators of the most outrageous of corrupt practices often seem completely unprepared for the backlash from their outraged honest colleagues.

The same psychiatrist explained: 'These corrupt officers appear to be acting as if they are a law unto themselves and often they don't even see themselves as crooked. But that's because they're suffering such underlying terror that they can't step back and look at what they are doing.

'As a result, they get very upset when there is a blacklash from their workmates. I think it's because many corrupt cops operate in such a small box they don't actually think outside that box about the consequences of their actions.'

There is also an expectation on the part of many crooked cops that they will escape justice by having their cases conveniently swept under the carpet to prevent embarrassing their superior officers, who'd prefer it if such corrupt practices were not revealed to the outside world.

No doubt the extraordinary success of *Line of Duty* is partly down to the 'shock factor' of the show. Police corruption still remains Britain's most undesirable – and unpublicised – crime. Yet over the past sixty years the UK has uncovered more corrupt police officers than anywhere else in the Western world.

Various reasons have contributed to the phenomenon of corrupt police: ever-shrinking police recruitment combined with large financial cutbacks by politicians. Also, officers are assigned away from the usual haunts of criminals, leaving the way clear for more crime and – with it – police corruption. Then there is the spiralling cost of living in the UK, which no doubt has pushed some once honest officers into breaking the law.

As one former London detective told me: 'That's no excuse. Law-abiding civilian citizens don't vault over the counter of a bank waving a gun and shouting, "Fill the bag!" just because they're under pressure at work and home. What on earth is admirable about betraying your colleagues and friends and even family?'

The real police themselves believe it's harder now than ever before to expose the activities of crooked cops in the UK. 'We have to tread so carefully these days. You can't just nab a bloke, sit him down and tell him we know what he's up to,' one retired detective recently explained.

Certainly, there are many rules in place today that prevent officers from pressurising an allegedly corrupt officer during an interview. But has this enabled many of those bad cops to slip through the net?

Instead of cleaning up the police, are all these rules and regulations helping bent cops to get away with breaking the law?

Successive UK governments have promised new funds and

laws to help 'smoke out' crooked police officers and duly punish them. But there is no sign of that happening in the immediate future.

Many in law enforcement believe that all suspected corrupt police officers should have their assets frozen until their court cases are fully heard. Some politicians have pledged to support this, but it's a definite case of easier said than done.

To date, only a small percentage of crooked police officers have been successfully prosecuted through the UK justice system. Some have even managed to keep their jobs, while others have quietly retired on a full pension provided by the taxpayer.

A succession of home secretaries have even pledged to target businesses and individuals linked to corrupt officers. But as one former south London detective explained from his £2 million retirement villa on the Mediterranean: 'The politicians are living in cloud cuckoo land. You're not going to stop corruption in the police by targeting people's businesses.'

A 2018 nationwide study into Britain's corrupt cops acknowledged that hundreds of crooked officers remain in their jobs and that isn't likely to change much over the next few years.

Police officers should look on corruption as something they're all just a few inches away from. The reality is that it seeps into every aspect of policing and the way the police respond to it is the key to whether officers become actually corrupt.

* * *

As a writer of true crime, I often come across stories that really are much stranger than fiction, as the saying goes. I've learned to understand and appreciate the multi-layered issues that so often lead to corruption amongst our so-called guardians of law and order.

Yet some real-life police detectives say they find the plotlines in *Line of Duty* too simplistic. 'The bad guy gets caught and dealt with, end of story. But it just isn't like that in real life,' said one recently retired south London detective. 'We don't always manage to put the bent cops away and that can be very frustrating.'

Meanwhile, the dramatic police world of *Line of Duty* goes from strength to strength.

As one executive from the series explained: 'The series manages to tread on that sensitive line between pro- and anti-police without banging a drum either way. Remember, *Line of Duty* is there to entertain an audience while the real police are there to make the public feel safe.'

SOURCES

This book has featured some of the most crooked cops in British criminal history. It's revealed the secrets behind the headlines and told why these criminals in uniform have gone down in the annals of underworld folklore.

But it is much more than just another true crime anthology. *Line of Duty: The Real Story* has hopefully helped highlight many fascinating characters on both sides of the law. No doubt many will have compared the characters of the hit TV show with the real crooked cops and the officers featured here. But in both the factual and fictional worlds, investigating a crooked cop requires the police to begrudgingly appreciate the 'art of bribery and corruption'. Where it comes from and why it happens.

The stories you've read here were recalled with insight and genuine emotion by many police officers on both sides of the law, who genuinely wanted to tell all. In some cases, they've spent the past thirty years ducking and diving through the underworld and now they want to finally come clean. I guess you could say they want closure.

Getting crooked policemen to co-operate *and* allow themselves to be identified in this book was a very tricky undertaking. Many corrupt cops even told me their 'straight' colleagues would come after them if they spoke publicly because no police officer likes to read about corruption in the force. So I was obliged to offer many of these sources a deal: talk to me openly and honestly and I will protect your identity. I suppose you could call it a literary version of the witness protection programme. But I granted them this special immunity because reproducing their stories is far more important than revealing their real names. *Line of Duty*'s success has also helped because it has brought so many questions to the surface when it comes to police corruption.

Some crooked police officers I spoke to demanded a fee for their help. I refused to give them a penny as that would have tainted what they had to say and put in doubt a lot of the facts I have recalled in this book. Much easier to ignore the greedy bent coppers and promise the others complete anonymity. That gave them the freedom to talk openly about sensitive information without living in fear of retribution.

But, of course, however I word this endnote I'm going to upset somebody. One of my main sources for this book put it bluntly: 'There are police officers out there who will be very pissed off that I've talked to you. They're nasty pieces of work and I don't want to upset *any* of them.'

Obviously, there are few readily available written records

covering many of the events outlined here, so I've had to trust the judgement and recollections of numerous individuals. Many were amongst those who did not want their names reproduced in this book. Therefore, much of what you have read here has been dependent on the memories of such men and women, fallible, contradictory, touched by pride, and capable of gross omission. But I believe them across the board because there are no hidden agendas in their stories, and I make no apologies for the strong language, either.

I have dramatised some events in this book because I did not want to expose the real suffering that people have been through because of the chilling world of police corruption. But overall, the dialogue represented in this book has been constructed from available documents, some was drawn from courtroom testimony, and some was reconstituted from the memory of those participants.

There is no doubt that corrupt police officers have perpetrated widespread and extreme acts of cruelty across the globe. And I can't always specifically depict those real acts of trauma in case that helps identify my sources or innocent parties. If the larger philosophical question is, Can we ever tell stories about police corruption that are not always factually accurate? I believe we can and should.

Much of the structure of this book relies on a long series of interviews, conversations, and recollections supplied, at times unwittingly, with dozens of individuals over many years. I've spent countless hours in formal (and informal) conversations with them.

Naturally, some of the missing real names will frustrate

those who have lived through the events mentioned here. But ultimately, I've tried to recreate stories of police corruption and its consequences, which have twisted and turned from the mean streets of London and the rest of this country to the criminal badlands of Spain's so-called Costa del Crime and then back to the UK.

No doubt I've missed out a few relevant characters. So, to those individuals I say sorry, although I'm not sure if any of them will mind!

To all the corrupt and honest police officers I've met down the years, I also say, 'Thank you.'

Without your help, this book would not have been possible.